Becky is an amazing young lady. Despite her disabilities, she can do and she does. Her words will appear from time to time in *My Voodoo* to remind us of the choices each of us always makes in how we view the world. Beautiful thoughts, from a beautiful person.

We had some tremendous feedback from *Corporate Voodoo*, and lots of requests for us to develop further some of the personal stuff. "How about me? How do I do this Voodoo magic?"

We now want to get personal. In order to get personal we need to get open and direct. We need to speak to you – not you, the General, Faceless Reader, but *you*, the you who is holding this book now. We want to share different perspectives on developing your self in these peculiar times[1]. Many movements are happening concurrently. Our worlds are shifting and moving faster and our values are not always in sync. Our parents are not always equipped to cope with the pace of change and act as advisors; they are certainly not the first port of call.

So where do we go to get advice and confidential help?

"I don't need the Samaritans yet, but it's not the Citizens Advice Bureau I'm looking for either. The priest is an interesting woman, my bank manager and doctor don't quite get it. Mystic Meg is not quite on the ball for me. My friends would not understand when I talk about my insecurities; we'd all laugh it away with the humour we always use to deflect the

---

[1] We have written a book for people first, and business second – but almost everyone works, and everyone deals with business (even if you just buy a cappuccino). You will therefore find references in this book to 'organisations', 'management', 'bosses' and other apparently work-specific concepts. Our advice is to use those references where you want them to be work-specific (for example if you are a leader in a company and are looking for some advice on how to energise your team). And ignore those references where they put you off. In other words, for 'organisation' read any social group you are a member of (e.g., family; club; band of friends); for 'leader', read any situation where you expect or are expected to have influence over others (e.g., you as parent; you as customer; you as community group member) and so on. The world of work is a rich source of learning for life, and vice versa – and that's why we don't separate out our advice.

uncomfortable. My work colleagues would see my asking for help as a sign of weakness. Anyway, this is personal, it is about me; maybe there's no need to even talk about this stuff. Sometimes when I do it hurts and gets me down for a couple of weeks… No one cares."

Until Voodoo, *My Voodoo*.

This book is designed and written for you to create your own advice space – a place for you to learn, face up, come clean, and move on. It will only deliver for you if you take it seriously enough to both complete and then maintain on a frequent basis.

In order to even attempt to improve our lives, we have to start by looking in the mirror. "Who am I? What am I good at? What are my strengths? What are my dreams?"

It is healthy to look in the mirror and feel both comfortable and pleased with who we are. *My Voodoo* is essentially a guide to getting comfortable with who we are, and being happy with our lives.

The future is the child of the present and the past; but the present and the past never recognise their own child when they stare it in the face.

In order to set the scene, think about freedom and what that actually means to you, and ask yourself what it is worth to you. Do we really value that we might actually just be free to be whom we want to be? Do we ever even pause in our breathless lives to consider why? Where to next? Do we feel the hot flush of confidence, excitement, urgency and passion? Do we know or feel how free we really can be?

What will inspire you to be free?

Last night I listened to, watched and read about the passing away of Queen Elizabeth, the Queen Mother. She was 101 years old, and the UK's most popular grandmother. She had lived all the way through the last century, and was admired and loved by many. One of her greatest moments was her decision not to abandon her home in London through the

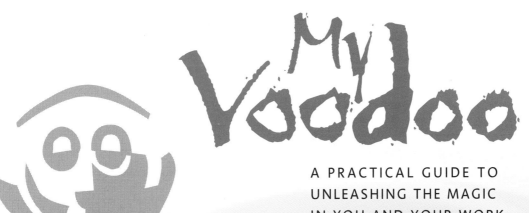

My Voodoo

A PRACTICAL GUIDE TO
UNLEASHING THE MAGIC
IN YOU AND YOUR WORK

DAVID FIRTH AND **RENE CARAYOL**

CAPSTONE

Copyright © David Firth & René Carayol, 2002

The right of David Firth & René Carayol to be identified as the author of this book has been asserted in accordance with the copyright, Designs and Patents Act 1988

First Published 2002 by
Capstone Publishing Limited (A Wiley Company)
8 Newtec Place
Magdalen Road
Oxford
OX4 1RE
United Kingdom
http://www.capstoneideas.com

All Rights Reserved. Exept for the quotation of small passages for the purposes of criticism and review, , no part of this publication may be reproduced, stored in a retrieval system or transmitted in any form or by any means, electronic, mechanical, photocopying, recording, scanning or otherwise, except under the terms of the Copyright, Designs and Patents Act 1988 or under the terms of a licence issued by the Copyright Licensing Agency Ltd, 90 Tottenham Court Road, London W1T 4LP, UK, without the permission in writing of the Publisher. Requests to the Publisher should be addressed to the Permissions Department, John Wiley & Sons Ltd, The Atrium, Southern Gate, Chichester, West Sussex PO19 8SQ, England, or emailed to permreq@wiley.co.uk, or faxed to (+44) 1243 770571.

Library of Congress Cataloging-in-Publication Data

A CIP catalogue record for this book is available from the British Library

ISBN 1- 84112-010-3

Designed and typeset by Baseline, Oxford
Printed and bound by Biddles Limited

Substantial discounts on bulk quantities of Capstone Books are available to corporations, professional associations and other organizations. For details telephone Capstone Publishing on (+44-1865-798623), fax (+44-1865-240941) or e-mail (info@wiley-capstone.co.uk)

Contents

Introduction: on opening   1

Part One: Voodoo asks: are you open?   12

Part Two: Voodoo asks: if you're open, what enters?   54

Part Three: Voodoo asks: are you finally going to turn over the closed sign?   84

Part Four: Voodoo connects   96

Part Five: Voodoo steps outside   152

Endpiece: Voodoo dreams   222

Preface

Foreword by David Butler, former Chairman, Butler Cox plc

Until quite recently the ethos that pervaded society was top down and paternalistic. The management style of nearly all organisations was modelled on a military command and control structure. And the same rigid rules governed the family and the community at large. Within living memory abortion was a criminal offence. There was no legislation on equal rights, and most working-class children left school at fourteen.

Nowhere was this oppressive style more evident than at work. At Unilever, in Africa House at Blackfriars, I once saw a card pinned to the organisation chart on the public announcement board.

Across this chart from root to crown
Ideas flow up and vetoes down.

What a sad story that told. A works engineer was once escorting me round a plant near Oxford. "We can burn a man out in four years," he said, with obvious pride.

Today we see such attitudes as socially dysfunctional. Yet these were the kinds of managers we then admired: go-getters, tough bastards. Those who accepted the top-down structure were equally prized; the men and women who would unswervingly follow instructions, even if it meant the Light Brigade charging the heavy artillery.

About thirty years ago something happened in the developed world that reformers had been waiting for since the days of Wells and Shaw. Universal education, imperfect as it was, began to bite. Workers were no longer prepared to accept as holy writ that the boss knew best. They began to ask a simple question: "Why?" The genie was out of the bottle. A whole generation of men and women has now grown up to question decisions imposed upon them from Olympus, whether the gods in question are bosses, government ministers, clerics or just Dad. On a bridge in Paris during the student uprising I saw a breathtaking graffito: "Be a realist. Demand the impossible."

As the idea of the iron-fisted boss went down the plughole, so too did the idea of the enterprise that pursued a steady and predictable path from one comfortable year to another. Even the largest and most successful companies now realise that they must reinvent themselves every few years to stay afloat. Markets are quick, fickle and unsentimental. And so, for better or worse, is society. Not for nothing were the men and women who grew up in the 1980s known as the 'me generation'. All certitude about societal norms vanished when the old order collapsed. Today we make up our moral code on the hoof. We have gained freedom, but lost certitude.

At work the demise of the command and control management philosophy left a black hole. If it is no longer the hallmark of a good manager that he can make people do what he wants – I use 'he' intentionally here – then what on earth is the hallmark?

In their book *Corporate Voodoo*, René Carayol and David Firth began to explore an alternative model. Voodoo is the belief in magic, that people and enterprises can transform themselves in unimaginable ways, that mavericks and magicians can steer the ship not by tracking its wake but by studying the stars, that since micro-management of intelligent workers is an impossibility, then inspired leadership may be the best bet, that sensible madness may be the way ahead.

Corporate Voodoo became a best-selling business book. I have seen some of the messages from readers testifying to its strange but undeniable eye-opening power. It unlocked dreams and made the unthinkable thinkable. And I have seen for myself the electrifying impact of the

Voodoo message when spelt out face to face by the authors, both in their very different ways dazzling orators. They are busily importing human values into the workplace, unleashing creativity, imagination and heart.

This new volume is intended to focus Voodoo on the more personal level. What can individuals do to set their magic free? It is, I believe, both a spellbinding read and a manifesto for another important step forward in the transformation and civilisation of work.

But be warned. It's also scary stuff, meant for scary people. The importance of Voodoo goes far beyond the workplace, to every aspect of human life.

Ah, sorry, what's that? You don't believe in magic. Fine. When you die and go to heaven, try telling Isaac Newton that a sub-atomic particle can be in two places at the same time, as we now know it can. He'll ask how. Tell him it's simple. The universe is made of magic, the cosmic overthrow of common sense.

David Butler

Welcome to
our book.
How's your
good self?

Let me tell you about
someone.

Becky Butler is the daughter of one of my closest friends. She has recently published her latest collection of poems, *The Unsure Promise*. Becky writes with imagination and feeling about our world and her perspective. There is something particularly Voodoo about her insights on our contemporary landscape. With Becky's permission, we have reprinted some of her stuff. It is *her* Voodoo.

INSIDE OUTSIDE

There you sit outside
the railings
Waiting for the bell to go
While the taunts of the
other children
Ring tunelessly in your ears.
"She's a thicko"
"She's a spastic"
"Can you understand me?"
"Nah, Course you can't!"
"Bet you don't even know
where you are!"
"Hey, Spazzo, you'll never
be one of us!"
"You can't even walk straight!"
"Well!" you want to shout,
"you're blind, the lot of you.
"Look inside who do you
really see?
I see a decent person,
One who is perfectly
normal,
One who hates teachers and
homework
Just like you."
Only difference is she can't walk.

Becky Butler

years of the Second World War, but to stay close and visible to the residents of the city. The bombing was constant, and the devastation colossal. 30,000 lives were lost in London alone. She was a constant and morale-boosting presence by her husband's side as they shared the pain of the nation.

Her selflessness, and her decision to go against both advice and protocol, served to endear her to a nation that needed heroes and heroines. Her desire for freedom gave much needed oxygen to a people who were in desperate need. The end result of her action was freedom. She played her part in our hour of need, and we will never forget.

A Voodoo inspiration can be dangerous. Anyone figuring the odds would run a mile. In 1940-41 many sensible and prudent people, some of them very high in British society, thought Britain should seek accommodation with Hitler, whereby we would keep the Empire and let Hitler take Europe. Surprisingly, Hitler was very interested in the possibility of such a deal. At a time when the USA was standing back, and the USSR was actually allied with Germany, supplying important elements of Germany's war material, Churchill did the crazy, civilisation-saving thing. All-out war, to the very end.

When JFK announced that the USA would make a moon landing within a decade, he can't have had the faintest idea whether it was possible. He set a heart-stopping target, and turned NASA loose. They would have died – some did – rather than fail. Uncertainty becomes the source of possibility.

A Voodoo inspiration can be controversial. When Beethoven's *Ninth Symphony* was first played in public, half the audience walked out. How can you have singers in a symphony? Today the same work provides the anthem for the European Union, and is probably the most performed work in the classical canon.

When Beckett's *Waiting for Godot* was first performed in Paris, half the audience left at the interval. In a recent poll run by the National Theatre, theatregoers voted the same play the most influential one of the twentieth century.

A Voodoo inspiration can be divisive. In his own lifetime Muhammad Ali went from being the most hated man in America to being the most loved. The man who was publicly vilified for cowardice raised the torch at the Olympics. How many Presidents of newly liberated countries can you think of who were labelled terrorists, often imprisoned as such? Try Nelson Mandela for a start.

A Voodoo inspiration can be courageous. David Beckham was once one of the most despised people in England, having been sent off in the crucial game for England at the 1998 World Cup against Argentina. Being sent off was not a hanging offence; it was the petulance, the apparently self-centred attitude and brat behaviour that got up people's noses. He was booed vociferously at most football grounds around the country.

He has continued to be true to himself and his family, despite many brickbats and the regular torrent of abuse. He has also become comfortable just being him. He has been appointed Captain of his country's football team, and we marvelled as his wonderful free-kick goal, at the last gasp against Greece, put England into the World Cup finals. It is much more the example he sets for life, rather than his massive example on the pitch and his outrageous natural ability, that makes Beckham yet another Voodoo practitioner.

Ali G asked Beckham's wife, Victoria, when her boy would start speaking properly; she answered "In a few years." When Ali G retorted "What about Brooklyn?" (their son), the nation laughed with them, not at them. Voodoo works.

A Voodoo inspiration can be magic.

The idea that we could have a child who escapes from the confines of the adult world and goes somewhere where he has power, both literally and metaphorically, really appealed to me.
J.K. Rowling

The author of the amazingly successful Harry Potter books has a true-life story that also has the magic of a fairy tale. Her inspiration for the writing of Harry Potter came to her when she was divorced, living on public assistance in a tiny Edinburgh flat with her infant daughter. The story goes that she wrote much of the initial Harry Potter book in a local café whilst her daughter slept at her side. The Scottish Arts Council provided her with a grant, which enabled her to finish the book.

When I was very low I had to achieve something. Without the challenge, I would have gone stark raving mad.

The rest is pure magic.

"Fascinating!" Mr Weasley would say, as Harry talked him through using a telephone. "Ingenious, really, how many ways Muggles have found of getting along without magic."
J.K. Rowling, Harry Potter and the Chamber of Secrets

A Voodoo Inspiration can be crazy. Back to Muhammad Ali. Who but Ali would ever think that the way to regain the world heavyweight championship is to confront one of the most destructive punchers in the history of the game, then let him hit you again and again and again until he's punched out, and you're still standing? And win.

There are indeed many stories of freedom that we could recount in this book. The only freedom story that really counts is yours.

To continue setting the scenes, I thought I might just share a few more thoughts and feelings about my personal inspiration, a great freedom fighter, and a serial Voodoo practitioner.

Honesty in a man is a vital characteristic; indeed it is the quintessential American trait. It was this quality that Ali embodied and which appealed to the American psyche. If this was indeed true, then it is tragically ironic that his honesty lost him the world heavyweight crown following his refusal to be drafted into the military. Ali declared that "I ain't got no quarrel with them Vietcong." Yet even in defeat, Ali demonstrated tremendous courage and grace under pressure. It is this that attracts Americans to Ali, regardless of race. Ali provided a distraction from the miasma of political corruption and showed the development of his political ideology. It could be argued that Ali's entry into the field of boxing saw the abandonment of the search for a 'white hope', as Ali was everyone's American. It is hard to analyse the appeal of Ali to different audiences, for each comes to look at him with their own personal history and agenda.

Clare Horrocks, Liverpool John Moores University

We would all like to believe that this courage was born out of necessity and oppression, and that in our new and civilised world, we are all free. Aren't we? Muhammad Ali was indeed courageous, but we do not need to be martyrs to the cause anymore. Oppression? We all do what we want to do, when we want to do it? Don't we? We have never had it so good. Have we?

How many people have heard the song 'You've got to search for the hero inside yourself...' without realising that it means them?

On my way back to 10 Downing Street, I am regularly greeted by protestors who are opposed to some of my thoughts and actions. This can be quite uncomfortable, but nowhere near as uncomfortable as them not having the freedom to voice their concerns and opposition.

Tony Blair

What is *your* Voodoo?

Voodoo asks: why wait for the future to happen when YOU create it NOW?

ONE WHO DOESN'T HAVE THE KEY

I have often wondered
What it would be like to be a child once more.
One who does not have the key,
The key to the world of beauty,
Of intrigue, of magic, of anguish,
Of fear, of hope,
Of love, of hate,
And so many other wonderful things
The world of books.

Becky Butler

Introduction

On opening

Opening the book

So what sort of book do you think this is? We don't mean 'How good do you think it is?' or 'What do you think of it so far?' because the answer to that last one in particular is, obviously, 'rubbish'. Like it always was, like it always will be. I was at a party recently in the old pub across the road from where I live in Yorkshire. The landlord interrupted the Karaoke at one point to ask, booming into the microphone: "What do you think of it so far?" To which we all cried "Rubbish!" Because that's the line. "Rubbish!" So he tried again. "What do you think of it so far?" And do you know what we said? That's right. "Rubbish!" Because that's the line. You can't not do it. Not if you know…[2]

What the landlord wanted to hear was "It's going pretty well, thank you, landlord", but we couldn't get out of the pattern, we were locked in by our history. Maybe he should have used a different form of words, and then we might have behaved differently.

---

[2] If you don't know, because you're too young or because you're American or something, have a look at the last page of the book.

So what do you think *that* little story was about (it's true, for what it's worth, although why I'm bothering to tell you that I don't know)? Come on, I'm serious, what do you think that story was about? What's its point?

I'll give you some space.

There'll be some space now, which is designed to encourage you to write down your answer to that question. Hah! Can you imagine it, the very thought – to *write it down*. But you won't, I know you, you're just like all the rest, you've been buying this sort of book – and we'll come back to that in a minute, I can assure you – for years and years and you've never written a single thing down; you just keep reading on, reading on, reading on, trying to get to the piece of information that will make a difference, to the idea that strikes you as new or different, to some content that will actually, you think, make a difference to your life – as if you're ever going to find it in a book.

Well, here is that space anyway, because this time you might just do as you're told, you might actually write the answer down in the space, and you might find out for yourself whether it really makes the difference that people claim – that writing stuff down on paper programmes your brain to assess, assimilate and eventually act on the words better than any mental exercise. But you won't.

So here is the space.

I'll remind you of the question:

What does that story about the landlord mean? In other words: why is it in the book?

So either you have written your answer or you haven't and you probably haven't. But that's OK. Maybe the space will act like a pause button anyway. Maybe in just those brief nano-seconds when your brain wasn't reading, after the word '… book?', maybe then there was a gap in that processing mind of yours. Just a thin sliver of, of … of openness.

Because that's what we'll be working with in this book. Your openness.

Fashionistas

I'm supposed to go back now to the answer to the question 'what does that story about the landlord mean?' I've set up a stream of thought, you see, and by rights I should follow the stream. I've already interrupted it by having this commentary about what I'm going on about, and I should, by rights, get back and keep on track. Otherwise you'll get distracted, you'll lose your way.

I'm supposed to say:

"Thanks for answering the question! What did you write? That it was about how conditioning pulls you into the past? If you did, that's right! Well done! Because it does. Let me show you what I mean. I was once speaking to a group out in Africa…" and then I'm supposed to tell you a made up story that reinforces the point and gets you to believe me and trust me and gets you to go "Hmm, seems as if this guy knows what he's talking about and I certainly resonate with that African story – he really seems to understand how I see the world…"

And if I don't do that, you'll get confused, bewildered even, and that will lead you inevitably to irritation (because that's how you are). You'll be beginning to resent me for not doing what your past conditioning about reading books tells you is right and proper. And then you'll end up taking the book back to the struggling book store where you bought it for a refund. Which won't do any of us any good.

Because books should be orderly, shouldn't they? Everything should be connected. Authors should make it easy for the reader to follow along, to get involved, to understand. And authors, particularly those who claim to be helping their reader, should be nice.

Business books, in particular, should be like businesses have been trying to be for ever: controlled and controlling, predictable, wary of the deviant. They should, shouldn't they?

Have you read *Corporate Voodoo*? This is the follow up. So have you read the first one? Did you see any of the reviews? We did. There's a nice person at Capstone who reads every publication that's ever published in the world and clips out anything related to the Capstone organisation, then distributes the right bits to the relevant authors.

A lot of these reviews said something about the style of the book, its structure and format. Not an easy read, they said (compared with others who thought it a a very easy read, but hey).

Well, we don't particularly want *My Voodoo* to be an 'easy read' either…

And we can anticipate the reaction that the current reviewers (and some readers) might have –

For example:

"It made me want to throw the book away!"

Here you might want to screw your face up like a little whining child and get the tone of voice right:

"They were horrible! How they think they can get anyone to want to lead them towards a magical change when they are being so crass and angry and arrogant themselves, I'll never know."

Well, never mind, we'll deal with those responses when we get them. But that will be our voodoo and not any one else's. The most important thing in this book is you, not us.

The most important thing in this book is you and the change you want to bring to your life and work, not us.

Voodoo: how a person responds to and creates the world

So...

stop waiting for us to tell you something you don't know already,

and get ready to think about why you aren't doing what you already know you should do...

Because in challenging your openness, we want to make you think, and if we have to make this read difficult and obtuse and stubborn in order to do that, then so be it.

Our intention is to wake you up – to get you to think and act for yourself – and we'll do that by any means necessary. What's important is that your life works.

What's not important is that you like us (nor any reviewer, nor potential purchaser of our consultancy for that matter).

Besides we're not going to get you to be a Maverick in your life by being Traditional and Normal ourselves, now are we?

Which box?

So what sort of book do you think this is? Where did you find it? In the Business section? General? Personal Development? In the Mind, Body, Spirit section? Bestsellers (hah!)? Which box does it fit in? Does it matter?

Which box do you want to work in?

YOU: MODEL ONE

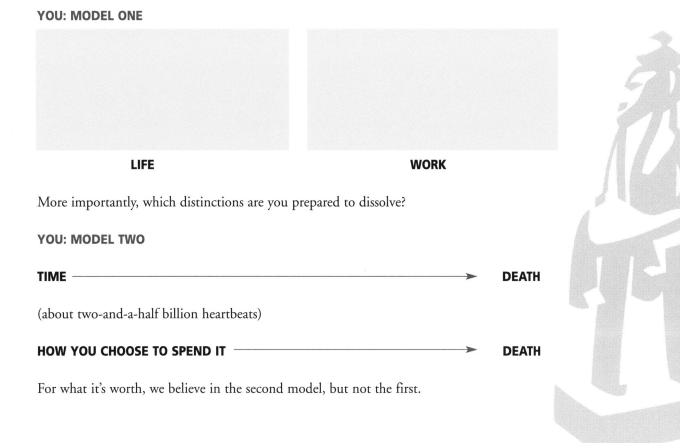

LIFE   WORK

More importantly, which distinctions are you prepared to dissolve?

YOU: MODEL TWO

TIME ⟶ **DEATH**

(about two-and-a-half billion heartbeats)

HOW YOU CHOOSE TO SPEND IT ⟶ **DEATH**

For what it's worth, we believe in the second model, but not the first.

REASONS PEOPLE DON'T WRITE IN THIS TYPE OF BOOK

1. they think they've got plenty of time
2. they want to keep the book clean
3. they are idle and lazy
4. they think they've done it all before
5. they wouldn't want anyone to see them doing it because they care about how they are seen and working on themselves is not something they'd ever own up to
6. they think they know what's going on in their heads
7. they're above it
8. they're too sussed to need to do it
9. they think that the voice inside their head is telling them the truth
10. they're trying to prove to the authors that they're in control
11. they're desperate to be right
12. they think that what they need to learn is somewhere in a book rather than in them

Write your reasons for not writing in a book of this type here:

Do I have to learn to tango?

I have before me now the 4 February 2002 edition of *Time* magazine, headlined 'A Look Ahead'. There's a backdrop of a blue sky, which is apt because this edition makes an attempt to predict 'the coming year's trends in Politics, Business and Culture'. The cover is a list of questions:

Will the recession end?
Can Bush stay popular?
Will there be a September 11 repeat?
Where's Bin Laden?
Is Arafat finished?
Can Chirac stay on top?
Will India and Pakistan nuke it out?
Will Schroder beat Stoiber?
Do I have to learn to tango?
Will oil stay cheap?
Will *The Lord of the Rings* top *Star Wars?*

What do you think has been going on in the world of business over the last couple of years? What do you think are the main themes of life and work from 2000 to the present day?

Write (or think) your answers here:

And what does all that require from you?

We think that it requires this –

A concentration on:

Your ability to understand and connect with other human beings
Your capacity for escaping the pull of the past
An understanding of the culture you help create
The extent to which you can embrace risk
Your ability to think the unthinkable
The ease with which you can be true to you
Your embracing of diversity
Your attitude to speed
Optimism
Courage
Your willingness to be, and your comfort in being, free…

All of that Voodoo and probably more.

OK? So that's the message of this whole introduction, really. All summed up, neat and tidy. You could have read just the last fifteen lines and got all you need to know. Because the rest had nothing to do with anything. Nothing to do with anything at all.

***OPEN** a. not closed or blocked up;*
allowing access; accessible to new ideas, unprejudiced; available
OXFORD ENGLISH DICTIONARY

Our companion volume, *Corporate Voodoo*, is sub-titled *'Principles for Business Mavericks and Magicians'.*

We feel more of us need to play both those roles if we are to bring some real magic into business and life.

During the writing of the book, we found out, almost by some magical accident, that the first two cards in any Tarot pack are these: the Fool (or Maverick) and the Magician.

The Fool

The FOOL is the wild card and represents the element of chance in a spread. As the beginning trump, he symbolizes the first step in a journey along a major path. You begin as the innocent Fool, ready to plunge into action with the attitude of folly. You find it impossible to see beyond the stimulus of total surprise, dropping into your life from the great nowhere and changing the course of events.

The FOOL reflects a spiritual consciousness rather than mere concern with material conditions. This card lends guidance through opportunity which falls into your hands. It indicates a need to leave things to fate, though it seems absurd; allowing coincidence and circumstance to lead to new and spontaneous directions.

The FOOL does not view life with great seriousness. Practical problems have no place in his cosmology. The FOOL lacks physical roots and does not worry about survival. He also leaves this to fate. The spirituality inherent in this card is without dogma. It speaks instead of deep divine treasures we carry within us, inherited from our human ancestry, which creates our inborn love of the natural world and curiosity about the great metaphysical truths which have fascinated people since the beginning of time.

The FOOL wanders the planet, ignorant to the pitfalls of life. He is unaware of disaster and barely acknowledges the dangers of existence. With no notion of self-protection, he often finds himself at the edge of a precipice, about to plunge off the surface of the planet. Even if something monumentally heavy happens, he does not consciously acknowledge it. The FOOL merely glances at the drama of life, accepting its face value.

www.tarotcam.com/deck/major/fool.html

The Magician

This card has the number 1, because it is the card of beginnings and everything you need for a good start: self-confidence, creativity, determination, willpower, self-control, skill, craft, purposeful action, energy, activity and vitality. It is the drive to choose your own direction, to realize your Self. Of course it is also the card of magick and the magician him- or herself, communicating between heaven and earth, thus creating and materializing new possibilities.

The MAGICIAN knows what he wants and works behind the scenes to procure his own ends. He appears in the least likely of places, moving quickly, private and secretive, keeping his presence as low-key as possible. He hides his method under the table and shifts his point of view so rapidly that nobody knows of his true intentions. He doesn't let others in on his plans as he does not want them to interfere with the success he seeks.

This trump often indicates a person who can be identified by his obsession with enhancing his power through manipulating appearances. His dialogue may be pre-designed to lead conversation towards his objective. Juggling the world around him, he plays games and competes for power, utilizing the utmost control, using high technology, sorcery and secrecy.

This card also depicts a genius for problem solving, the ability to create change, gaining mastery over your environment, controlling your own life, channelling the spectrum of sensation and movement into categories of scientific dimensions. The MAGICIAN has the ability to tap into the universal force and bring whatever energy he finds to his orbit.
www.tarotcam.com/deck/major/magician.html

So the Fool is the big zero, the everything and nothing, the big 'who knows what might happen?', the big Possibility. Biting at his heels is the little dog of opportunity. Above him the stars. Below him the rocks. Either destination can be reached – and either of them only by moving forwards.

The Fool, or Maverick, in us keeps us curious and in awe of what might be possible…

And the Magician is the one who can make things happen, who can bring things into being that apparently were not there before – just like a rabbit out of an empty hat. With one hand pointing to the heavens, and the other to the earth, he makes the ethereal manifest.

The Magician in us can make our dreams real.

Together the two roles are a powerful combination.

> **This book is designed to develop your capacity**
> **for being both a Maverick and a Magician**
>
> **so that you can continue to be open to what might be possible for you**
>
> **(rather than live a life closed down by your past conditioning)**
>
> **and so that you can design and create a life that matters to you**
>
> **(rather than accept the existence that life has handed you).**

But let's get a couple of things straight first...

1. voodoo asks: are you open to magic?

When we wrote *Corporate Voodoo*, we made play of the fact that it coincided with the Harry Potter phenomenon. We called our Fast businesses – those that seemed to have the right ingredients to conjure up amazing performances in the business world, such as Orange, Tesco, Vodafone – Initiates. And we called our Slow businesses Muggles (for example BT, M&S, John Lewis).

A reviewer from London's *Daily Telegraph* said that we were 'jumping on the Potter bandwagon'. So she'll be delighted to see that, later in this book, we'll be drawing on imagery associated with *The Lord of the Rings* too. But that's just us, through and through, not a creative thought in our heads.

Yet if people keep bringing out major works about sorcery, and if people in their record-breaking millions across the globe keep reading them and going to see films of them, then we'll have to keep drawing the conclusion that there's something in the zeitgeist about magic. And whilst it's here, we choose to be interested in why.

[Oh, and that chap Philip Pullman, who just won the Whitbread prize for *The Amber Spyglass*. First time a 'book for children' has been so honoured. Fantasy book. Magic. Sorcery.]

Now here's a thought.

Why shouldn't business be reconfigured as a place of magic? Can the magical zeitgeist encompass the world of work? Well, why not? For too long, the culture's core beliefs about business have been to do with rapaciousness, greed, environmental and communal ruin, excess, corruption and lies. And at its best, a place of glamour, large pay rises, short-termism, big cars, sharp suits, corner offices, excess, corruption and lies. That's why as we go to press, the vultures are out feeding on Enron. Probably a place that majored in all those vices, who knows, but it certainly feels good to be kicking a good old-fashioned Nasty Company again, doesn't it – and we even get to blame the accountants too – after a couple of lean years of having only those crazy dotcoms to mock, with their strange seating arrangements and high idealism?

Whatever, we love to hate our work, we love to be suspicious of our companies.

Now I don't know about you, but personally I've met very few leaders who were corrupt, avaricious or deceitful. I've met loads of people who think that their boss is all of those things, just like all those people who think their business is only concerned with the bottom line – but it's usually myth-making. Making up monsters is how people protect themselves from the really scary realisation that there's nothing under the bed. And then they find themselves on their own in the dark, staring up at the ceiling.

I think that's even worse, the fact that Evil Business is all in our heads. I think that's an even worse reflection on humanity – not that it created Business evil, but that it wanted to find it so.

So we'd like you to be truly maverick, and join us in stepping out of the tribe that tells us that business is evil.

We believe we can make business magical.

Think about it. What's all that Potter, Tolkien, Pullman stuff about?

Perhaps:

◆ a fascination with the unexplainable
◆ an attraction to the invisible
◆ a focus on questing, making a stand for something, doing something extraordinary, being heroic, having a purpose
◆ a need for escape – a pull towards storytelling

So it is with business and our lives in business.

We assert that all of the 'benefits' listed above, which this renewed passion for fantasy literature seems to offer, are available in the business world today:

A fascination with the unexplainable:
this is the age of difficulty, of complexity, of paradox in business, of huge, downright confusing change; and with that comes the rise of experimentation, of innovation, of 'no one right answer'. Since nobody can claim to have the right answer, being in business is not a closed club any more. We've all got a chance to have a go…

An attraction to the invisible:
never before has the individual human being, the unit of one, mattered more in an organisation; not as a human resource, but as the only conduit for creativity and ideas. And

with the individuals come all those 'invisible' traits which companies are realising they need: passion, trust, loyalty (howsoever brief), love…

A focus on questing, making a stand for something, doing something extraordinary, being heroic, having a purpose:
this is a time when more and more people are allowed to talk about the fact that work is an important part of our life, and not just because it pays the bills. Our work is an expression of who we are; how we choose to work in the world creates our destiny. What do you choose? Another day, another dollar? Or something more?

A need for escape – a pull towards storytelling:
and as soon as you leave the shallow inevitability of the world where you're only in it for the money, you enter a new story that you find you can create.

The thing about making business magical is that we don't start with the government, we don't start with Enron, we don't start with your boss even.

We start with you.

And that's why we've written this book. For you.

And in order to do that, in order to make that change, you've got to give up on some old beliefs about business, about work, about organisations – and about yourself. You'll have to give up on the conditioning that is the inevitable consequence of those old beliefs. You'll have to stop being a reflex. You'll have to stop saying "Rubbish!" when someone asks "What do you think of it so far?"

EXERCISE

They say that, one Sunday, they burnt some Harry Potter books at a church in Pennsylvania…

What does that make you think about
- the burners
- the books
- what this book might be about for you?

What does magic look like?

Magic produces surprising results. There's a priceless moment in one of the David Blaine TV specials when he produces the 'right' card from some impossible place. A little boy, the subject of this sleight of hand, stares open-mouthed at Blaine for long seconds afterwards; you can see his lips twitching as if he wants to speak, but there's nothing coming out. In the end he begins to cry, so freaked is he by his experience…

Now that's surprising!

What would surprising results be for you? You'll be tempted to think of fantasy items – and yes, it would be surprising to win the lottery, it would be surprising to wake up tomorrow as slim and beautiful and sexy as you were fifteen years ago.

Funnily enough, we cannot guarantee you these results. Instead we ask you to look closely at your life and work, and at all those areas where – if only you and other people thought, talked and acted somewhat differently – the results would be surprising, and even magical. There are many aspects of life which are the opposite of magical – mundane, dull, stupified, complacent, closed – and we accept them as being so, never thinking there could be any other way.

Think of 'surprising results' at work.

◆ What if it was a joy to work at your company because you were proud of its service to the world and of your contribution to it?

◆ What if your organisation was able to generate significant wealth without your thinking that wealth was only available to a small minority?

◆ What if your company was really able to live its values rather than have them etched on a plaque – wouldn't that be magical?

◆ What if your organisation communicated freely and openly, and knowledge was shared and understood by all?

◆ What if you were able to resolve upsets and conflicts without judgement and blame, rather than resorting to bitching, backstabbing and rumour-mongering?

◆ What if your team was consistently able to generate creative solutions to the challenges it faced, and the generation of those solutions was a fun experience?

This book provides some of the tools, processes, behaviours and attitudes that would generate such magic.

In order for us to have magical lives, we don't need fantasy. We need to work at transmuting the dross around us into something that we know we ought to have, something we deserve to have, something deep down that we know we could have.

And transmuting that dross, we repeat, starts with you… Change you and we'll change your whole world. You helped make the dross, so you can create the magic.

GENERATING MAGIC

Try:

- Giving up your need to be right

- Giving up the fantasy that you can, one day, if you work hard enough, be invincible

- Giving up your need to get something

- Giving more and asking for less in return

- Stopping worrying about what your values could be; observe yourself in action and you'll know what your values are

- Cultivating a relationship with the best, most trustworthy voices inside you; get to recognise the voices in you that you don't trust, and ignore them

- Showing up, whenever you are, where ever you are. Whatever you have to do, howsoever humdrum, do it to the best of your abilities

- Being curious about how things turn out around you. Try for understanding rather than judgement

- Being willing for magic to happen, rather than trying your best to will it to happen

Listen:
WE'LL ASK AGAIN:
ARE YOU REALLY OPEN TO MAGIC?

Magic happens

Our lives and careers can and must be influenced by us. This does involve taking a large and difficult amount of responsibility for who we are and what we do. This is not easy. Especially when set against our prevalent cultural viewpoint that we are uncomfortable with change, especially when it involves pushing ourselves a little forward. It really does start with an honest self-appraisal. Most of us have had feedback from a number of different sources about what we are good at and our areas for improvement. Parents, teachers, managers, colleagues, friends and family are forever approving and disapproving. What is our view? Whose feedback is most helpful?

Environments and atmospheres can be massively constraining for magic, or they can provide the necessary oxygen that encourages magic to happen. Think about where you spend your thinking and reflecting time. Think who you have around you when you are soul-searching and problem solving. How does the scenery make you feel? How supportive are the people you have chosen to be around?

Balls

We do not normally think about having Vinnie Jones (the hardest of hard professional footballers) and magic in the same sentence. Vinnie came from the school of hard knocks; some would say that he was the school of hard knocks. Who could ever forget the great sporting photo and icon of the early 90s when Vinnie had a chubby Gazza's testicles firmly clenched in his left hand? It was his snarling face and Gazza's obvious pain that are etched in our minds. Vinnie was the epitome of blue-collar anger; he appeared to hate everyone, and he was at his most eloquent when he was at his most muscular.

His education was on the streets of tough London. His life appeared to be mapped out already. He was a hod carrier on a building site. Vinnie was never going to allow it to end there; he could play football and was soon professional. He became famous and played important roles for some big football clubs in England. He was known for his unbridled aggression and as a stopper of the most brutal order. As his career started to draw to a close, the huge athleticism that made him more fearsome than Anne Robinson started to wane. He was human after all. But what came next?

Vinnie had one overriding ambition, to become a movie star. He had fulfilled one dream, to become a professional footballer, against all the odds. He started hanging around with actors, TV, stage or Hollywood; surprisingly Vinnie rubbed shoulders, not shins, with them. His break came when the fashionable English director, Guy Ritchie, needed a Cockney 'hard nut'. *Lock, Stock and Two Smoking Barrels* has become a cult hit. Vinnie played a blinder. There is a massive scene in which Vinnie's character was asked to lose it. In fact Guy Ritchie asked Vinnie whether he could do malice. "Yeah, I can do that," Vinnie replied. Guy started to explain in detail what he was after, Vinnie cut in "I can do malice". The scene was shot in near disbelief and palpable fear. Vinnie had cause to smash someone's head in using a car door. It was frightening and there was no way anybody was going to say that it needed a second cut. Guy called a break as everybody on the set was shaken and in awe of what they had just witnessed.

Vinnie was on his way to becoming a movie star. A snarling and uncompromising movie star.

Errol Flynn was a movie star; Humphrey Bogart was a movie star, as was John Wayne. Tom Cruise, Arnold Schwarzenegger and Bruce Willis are all great movie stars. There is something about them that will always be box office. Robert de Niro, Al Pacino and Dustin Hoffman are all great actors, but not necessarily great movie stars. What is this indefinable quality that all movie stars have? I am not sure exactly what it is, but it has something to do with desire. Vinnie has it.

Vinnie has magic. He knows what he is good at, and he knows what he wants. He knows the difference between a negative and a positive environment. He chooses his friends and companions carefully. He wants to win and is comfortable feeling that way.

Many of us may have massive issues with the way Vinnie carries himself. We may disagree with the characters he has played, both on the football pitch and on film. We may not care for someone who is at his best when snarling and cussing.

We can all admire his magic.

So back to us. What can we take from Vinnie's approach? He really understood his strengths and how to exploit and capitalise upon them. He did this admirably. He reached and achieved all his goals as footballer. His relationship with his wife, Tanya, has been a source of inspiration for him. He has employed an old school friend as his personal assistant and they get on as well now as they did then (they still swap a few right-handers occasionally, but what the hell). He prides himself on not forgetting people that have been loyal and faithful to him. On a recent filming trip to Los Angeles, many friends and family came over to spend days with Vinnie and Tanya in LA.

He has had the Hollywood break. He appeared alongside Nicolas Cage in *Gone in 60 Seconds*. He is now starring in the aptly named *Mean Machine*.

Vinnie is obviously a hard act to follow, but learn from him we can. A real Voodoo hero.

And here's another one

Kids Company
Camila Batmanghelidjh is the founder and director of the charity Kids Company. She founded the charity in 1996 in response to the growing number of children who do not have the advantages of a stable home life, love and attention. Camila was born into an aristocratic family with all the usual trappings and favours, but that's not the story. She is from Iran, or Persia as it was then. Camila left her country of birth at the age of nine and moved to the UK. She has always had the vision of building an organisation that helped and assisted the abused children of our world. Somehow this feels as though she had seen oppression and helplessness at close hand, but she is beautifully aspirational and optimistic.
She really comes into her own when the kids of Kids Company surround her. These are sometimes children of the street, who are used to having to be tough and resilient, where

displays of feelings and emotions are seen as signs of weakness. They are completely different around Camila. They value and love her and they really do know how special she really is in their dark world. Camila was taken to court by her building society because she stopped paying her mortgage. She had used the money to start Kids Company.

She is a trained psychotherapist who is living her dream, and it is a dream. The good she does is instructive for all of us; like Vinnie Jones she has desire. Like Vinnie she was not going to be denied. Like Vinnie, she is doing what she wants to do. Like Vinnie, many said she could never do that. Like Vinnie she has Voodoo.

She has taken the decision not to have children as she feels it will be impossible for her to tear herself away from the children she already has at Kids Company, and it would not be fair. This remarkable woman had a dream of assisting those who were without help or understanding. We all have it within us to understand and appreciate her contribution. On reading the information sheet from Kids Company, I… well, you read it.

KIDS COMPANY

Kids Company is a registered charity (no: 1068298) offering support to exceptionally vulnerable children who need both therapeutic and practical help. We support children whose parents are unable to care for them due to their own difficulties. Many of the children have been physically and sexually abused. Some have to become carers to younger siblings as their parents cope with addiction and mental health problems. Some children have resorted to prostitution and crime as a means of supporting their households.

The extreme cases of abuse receive some support from Social Services, but 90% of our children are invisible to services, often receiving inadequate care and having to manage difficulties on their own.

With fragile psychological states they face relentless trauma. Some children are resilient and survive with minimum distortions of feelings; the more vulnerable ones shut down their capacities to feel in order to minimise the pain and helplessness. Years of 'emotional shutdown' result in losing the capacity to empathise and may render the child into a state of 'lethal coldness'.

Void of feelings most of these children are capable of causing great harm. They hurt people, damage properties and escalate into detachment in the context of which they recognise no love, honour or loyalty. These aggressive and destructive children unfortunately make it very difficult for people to like or feel compassion for them. Yet these, along with the introverted, are the very children who refer themselves to our services.

Kids Company has been able to reach and engage children whose needs present multiple challenges. We deliver our work by offering a range of services in schools as well as at our Children's Centre (The Arches).

Talent
Kids Company is 'For Children by Children' with many special adults making it possible through their generous support.

The poem below describes a journey many of our children make: from being rejected and feeling worthless to discovering their strengths. Often we cannot change their daily lives but we can build up their resilience and in our love show them hope for a better future.

The boy who wrote this poem was initially presented as exceptionally withdrawn. One of triplets, his head was distorted in shape and often hidden beneath a hood. He has been rejected by his mother who abused him. He was left in local authority care where he felt no one loved him. Since joining Kids Company he has thrived and no longer feels a need to hide.

Darrnel's Poem

Squashed up for nine months
All three of us
You kept us warm, you fed us, you talked to us
We heard your sweet voice
Whilst we laid in the dark
You pushed us out
Me, then him, six hours later you had the last
You gave us life, you watched us live, you watched us grow.

We, all three, turned to the ripe tender age of 8
The age of experiments
The age of developments
Did I thrive? No
What did I learn?
I'm different why? I don't know
How I don't know
But you showed me
I felt the pain, the hurt
I cried once, but no more
You will not see the tears any more
They will stay within

Why do you love them and not me?
What did I do wrong?
You say I'm bad, but I know I'm not

I want to go
I have to go before you kill me
But I want to stay

Now I've gone you haven't changed
You still haunt me, with your threats that enter my dreams
I'm all alone now

Still wondering. When did it all go wrong?
I'm sorry mum, for all I did wrong
I'm sorry mum, for being bad
I'm sorry mum, for telling the police
I'm sorry mum, for letting our family secret out
But most of all I'm sorry for believing you
For I am loveable, I am strong, and I will succeed as
I am the greatest Darrnel
And you cannot touch me now.

Darrnel, *aged 13*

Case Studies

The following case studies illustrate some of the children we deal with on a daily basis. They are chosen not because they are shocking but because they represent the kinds of traumatic experiences our children have coped with.

Female aged 14; Male aged 12; Male aged 11; and Female aged 7: Social services have a report from a member of the public who saw the eldest girl (at the time aged 7) scavenging in bins for food. She was carrying two younger children (her brothers). The children's father is a drug addict; he took her at age 13 on a burglary just before Christmas and they were caught. He received a three-year prison sentence and the children were left with their mother who was also a drug addict. In pursuit of her fix she went to a dealer's house with her 7-year-old daughter, a gunman broke in and threw the dealer out of the window to his near death. The 7 year old would not stop crying for days. These children had been out of school for nearly two years. Drug dealers and addicts frequent their house giving the home an atmosphere of bizarreness and danger. The children have few clothes and are barely washed; they are often hungry and bewildered. To attempt to meet their needs the eldest girl sank into prostitution; with this money she would feed her brothers and sister, and sometimes buy heroin for her mother. On two occasions she has been raped and has contracted sexually transmitted diseases.

Male aged 11; male aged 9; Female aged 8; Female aged 7; female aged 6; male aged 18 months: The children's fathers have all disappeared. Their mother was sexually abused by her own father who is also thought to have sexually abused the 8-year-old girl. The 7 year old is physically severely damaged as at the age of two she was left in care of a man who assaulted her using his penis and a set of keys, which tore her vagina badly. She does not yet know what has happened to her. The 11-year-old boy has severe specific learning difficulties. He is very vulnerable and presents like an old man who has the burdens of the world on his shoulders; he does not attend school. The 6 year old's father appears from time to time but has a drug and alcohol problem. He batters the mother and bullies the children. The children are all very unkempt and deprived.

Work In Schools
Usually a school asks us in. We provide therapeutic support in the form of one-to-one counselling; group work around specialist topics, e.g. bullying or bereavement; children with special educational needs are offered classroom support or extra tuition. Whole classes are offered Arts and Sports activities as well as self-esteem programmes.

We bring in companies from the City to help change the school environment, e.g. one hundred Accenture employees painted a school from top to bottom in five hours. Goldman Sachs volunteers created a beautiful playground in a day. Approximately 4000 children per week take up a number of these services, some of them attending more than one programme. Postgraduate volunteers, who are supervised weekly, deliver most of our work in schools.

Schools who have made use of the project describe a positive change in the school, with greater calm and an enhanced sense of creativity. Children self-refer to our services.

Work at the Arches
Six railway arches, donated by Spacia, house a thriving centre offering six days per week support to exceptionally vulnerable children. We have three social workers, four specialist teachers, psychotherapists, a child psychiatrist, sports and arts facilitators. Currently forty staff in total.

Children are offered three meals a day, clothes, help with school uniform, bedding and all other necessities. Children are taken to the dentist, optician and sexual health clinic. Our staff represent them at meetings with outside agencies including schools and training programmes. During the day children who have no school placements are offered full time education paid for by Lambeth and Southwark Education Authorities or individual schools. After school the same teachers help children who have school placements with homework and reading. Our intervention means children are offered access to appropriate educational support especially in the absence of parents who advocate on their behalf.

Our adolescents are offered a post-16 programme that includes employment and training support via our new 'Job Club' supported by Comic Relief.

For children with a history of criminal involvement we facilitate a Youth Offending Package currently funded by the Youth Justice Board.

Our philosophy promotes respect, love and the return to children of a dignity which is their birthright. Everyday our children are a challenge and an inspiration.

Kids Company relies on donations so, if you are able to share in the support of our children, please contact either: Camila Batmanghelidjh or Diane Flatt on 020 7703 1808, or write to: Kids Company, Arch 259 Grosvenor Court, Grosvenor Terrace, London SE5 0NP.
www.kidsco.org.uk

Voodoo says: honour the children, Kids Company and Camila

Founder Camila Batmanghelidjh, who worked with police on the Damilola Taylor murder investigation, says:

"If people knew about the lives some children have and why they turn to gangs for solidarity, they'd be horrified. We'd intended the service to cater for the under-11s. But on our opening around 100 African/Caribbean adolescent boys came to 'check us out'. They were from gangs, they had weapons and enough anger and sarcasm to challenge all of us. Now we work with them to discover and nurture their talents and interests. Reached early, children's belief in tenderness and humanity can be restored."

Camila founded this unique charity, paid for entirely by her own fund-raising, in 1996. It currently offers support to 1,600 children a week and occupies six brightly painted railway arches. As well as being a free after-school club, Kids Company also offers education to persistent truants so difficult that no conventional school will take them.

"Within weeks of opening, children were waiting at the gates in the morning and didn't want to leave at night," says Camila. "Every day, between 40 and 150 children turn up. Most of them heard about us through friends."

Vinnie Jones and Camila Batmanghelidjh, doing what works for them. Doing what they enjoy. Because they enjoy it, they are doing it with huge passion, and they are good at it. It's not orthodox, it's not easy, but it is them and it is real. The magic is real.

You may not like Vinnie Jones, or his work, or his being an example in a book like this. He's hardly Gandhi or Bill Gates, now is is he?

But he made magic happen in his life. Transformation took place. He asked the Fool's question 'Why not..?' And then he used the Magician's art to take the dream and manifest it in reality.

If him, why not you?

Maybe you're more comfortable with Camila. One Voodoo story is of a man working out of an ordinary background into the LA sunshine; the other a woman who leaves her privileged background to one side in order to benefit the lives of others.

They are both the same story: Voodoo says your identity is your future, but that does not have to mean that your history is your future.

Magic happens when you leave the past behind.

THE MIRROR

There I sit, staring into the mirror of my mind.
The reflection is the same as its always been,
A teenage girl – little different from any other.
But then I look.
And I see a different face.
The same girl –
Only this time she is much younger.
Then I look a third time
And I see a disfigured monster
A monster who is partly the teenage girl
And partly the young child.
I can hear them now
Arguing – "You stupid fool –
Of course you'll have a brilliant time
Once you get there!"
The other voice, retaliating
"But I've never done it before –
I'll miss them…Aaaargh!"
"You've got to make the break,
You're fifteen for goodness sake!"
Make the break – fifteen – miss them,
Oh God
Why can't I see one face?
One side of the mirror?
Why am I stuck in the middle?

Becky Butler

GENERATING MAGIC: YOUR TURN

Try:

Giving up your need to be right
If I gave up my need to be right, what might happen...?

Giving up your need to get something
If I let go of depending, what might happen..?

Giving up the fantasy that you can, one day, if you work hard enough, be invincible
If I accepted myself just as I am, what might happen..?

Giving more and asking for less in return
If I did more in a spirit of service, what might happen..?

Cultivating a relationship with the best, most trustworthy voices inside you; get to recognise the voices in you that you don't trust
If I listened to the best part of myself more, what would I hear..?

Being curious about how things turn out around you. Try for understanding rather than judgement
If I judged less, what might happen..?

Showing up, whenever you are, wherever you are. Whatever you have to do, howsoever humdrum, do it to the best of your abilities
If I hid less behind boredom, cynicism or impatience, what might I find..?

Being willing for magic to happen, rather than trying your best to will it to happen
If I let go more, what might happen..?

Thank you.

2. Voodoo asks: Are you ready for freedom?

To be open to magic you've got to be free to suspend your (dis)belief. The (dis)belief that you're not worth it, that it could never happen to you, that it's not your turn, that someone else is stopping you, that something else is getting in the way. You've got to suspend your (dis)belief that you're not free.

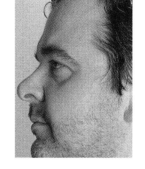

Now to get to such a place of freedom, you've probably got to free yourself from your beliefs about freedom.

Do you have any of these beliefs?

That those at the top of the organisation are free, and you are not

That those on the outside of your organisation are free and you are not

That money makes you free (go on, you really believe that one, don't you?)

That freedom is for gurus; pragmatists have to make tradeoffs

That…

That…

What is freedom? It's the freedom to know and then express your power, your identity and your purpose.

And the irony is, you're never not free.

You are free to be powerless, to be confused, to be unclear. If you choose it. Many people make that choice all their lives and justify it by thinking that they're trapped. Powerless is an identity – and you can live into that just as you can live into the identity of Powerful. Cynical is a purpose, just like Transformation, or Growth, or Money, or Love.

You have no obligations. In the morning you'll have breakfast with your children and then you'll be off to work. And then you'll come back to them. And you'll think you do that because you have to, because you have responsibilities. Because you're not free. No; wrong. You choose to come home. And you choose where and how you spend your time up between breakfast and death.

What's life about? You shape it a bit, you respond to it a bit. That's all and that's everything. Deepen your ability to shape your life (as far as you can), extend your capacity to respond to life (as well as you are able), and you'll be as near to happy as we know. But understand one thing. Let's say there was a shaping/responding effectiveness scale from one to ten. Hitting one takes as much freedom as hitting ten. The only difference is the influence that comes from consciousness, from being awake to your freedom and what else you could do with it (as opposed to being asleep and squandering it all).

INEVITABILITY AND FREEDOM

I worked with a company recently that was trying to do a big cultural change programme that would match and align the organisation with a radically changing world. They had been, in effect, a big agency for the financial world, someone employed by banks to serve the banks. Everyone threw into a pot to pay them, and this agency did their job.

And then things changed, and the free market waltzed in on them. The financial world changed their relationship with them, the big pot of money disappeared. My client began to understand what this competition thing was that everyone else had been talking about for so long.

The cultural change my client was facing was similar to the (dis)belief change that anyone goes through when they want some magic in their lives. It's the change which moves you out of inevitability and into freedom. For my client, everything had been inevitable. It was inevitable that they'd be able to pay themselves good salaries, because there was no competition to provide a benchmark. It was inevitable that there was little participation in decision-making; there was no need. Inside the glass bubble of the business relationship, there was no complexity to face that would warrant tapping into the collective wisdom of the employees. There was no need for much in the way of innovation. And so when the fantasy of inevitability collapsed, the company was left as free as it always had been in truth, but with the organisational equivalent of stiff joints, atrophied muscles and brittle bones. They didn't realise how bad they felt until they came squinting out of jail and into the bright light outside…

So too with the individual. Living a life of inevitability, of no choice, of obligation, tires you out, no matter how luxurious the jail. How fit for freedom are you?

Our organisations are complicit in maintaining the fantasy that we're indentured to them, but complicit is a two way street. It's like nicotine addiction. On one side cigarette marketing reinforces how much we need it; on the other, we tell ourselves how hard it will be to give it up. And so we continue to freely choose addiction. We can open the cell door by changing how we think.

Complicity is also in the environment that we live and work in – and if you're truly ready for freedom you'll have to be prepared to leave the tribe. Continuing to say yes to the colleagues who tell you how oppressed you all are by your bad boss is not an embracing of community, it's an addiction sustained by the dealer.

Leaving does not have to mean exiting the organisation (or the group, or the family). If you choose to stay – perhaps because you've realised that your company may not be the best place for you in the future, but is an excellent training laboratory for you in the present – then being free means thinking and speaking for yourself. Make your own mind up. See your world as it really is, not how it is presented to you, either by your leaders or your peers…

There are freedom issues all around us, every day. Here's another take on the same theme…

EXERCISE

How I react when someone tells me I'm free is this: I say…	I get a physical reaction in my body somewhere like this…
My face makes this expression…	It makes me think of…
	And after a while, all that makes me feel…

Thank you.

THE EURO AND FREEDOM: IT'S NOT JUST ABOUT MONEY

On a Radio Five Live phone in on New Years Day, I got drawn into a discussion about the Euro. I say 'a discussion', but that's being too polite. What happened was that two sets of people with diametrically opposing views just restated their entrenched opinions for the hundredth time, on the radio instead of in the saloon bar. Almost all the points made centred exclusively on the financial questions, the benefits and risks for UK plc in joining the Euro or staying out. However hard the compère, Nicky Campbell, tried to get people to think about wider issues, the callers all harked back to the same question: "What's in it for us, money-wise?"

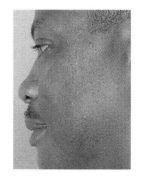

Those who were against joining the Euro made a few feeble attempts to depict unfavourable financial consequences. But at root their objection is not financial, not even political, but traditional. They feel that the EU process has gone far enough. Prompted by crazy European directives such as the permitted curvature of bananas – and I'm sure some of these are invented in El Vino's – they've had European integration up to here. If we wanted to be governed from Europe, we might as well have lost World War II, that would have done the trick. Statue of Adolf Hitler in Parliament Square? Why ever not?

Those callers (the minority) who were in favour of Britain joining the Euro zone were at heart backing a political crusade. They haven't calculated the financial niceties of membership any more than the sceptics. They just feel that the drive to make Europe as big a hitter on the world stage as Uncle Sam is, as Japan was, and as China will be, justifies a financial risk or two. They have a dream in which Mr Greenspan listens to us.

There is a massive process of self-deception at work here. We all talk as if the financial arguments are the key to the whole debate. But in reality it's a bunch of emotive, irrational, inchoate hopes and fears about an unknown and unknowable future that shape our attitudes. Our beloved Chancellor has said that it's the five economic criteria that will make all the difference. If they are met, the government will recommend a yes vote in a referendum, otherwise not. Let me tell you a secret. The five criteria are largely mythical. They are so vague and subjective that any economist could make a case for or against on precisely the same data, just to suit whoever asked for it. A Treasury official, too candid for his own good, recently admitted that the five criteria are largely subjective. And – the clincher – can anyone except Gordon Brown ever remember exactly what they are?

There is a specific UK overlay to all of this. People often boast about the much-vaunted stability of our system of governance. I saw a wonderful cartoon once. It was the demonstration of the moderates. They were chanting, "What do we want? Gradual change! When do we want it? In due course…" This is funny, but for UK plc also tragically revealing. In a jet-speed world we are still travelling in a horse and cart. There are innumerable examples of British decision taking that make a torpid snail look like Maurice Greene. Our laws take forever to change, initiatives are buried under a mountain of Law Commission reports, green papers, white papers, draft bills, bills. It's lucky the Queen has been around for so long, otherwise she probably wouldn't have signed more than a handful of acts into law. The railways, the NHS, the London transport system, immigration law, there are dozens of important areas of national life where we've been, quite honestly, faffing about for decades.

Our planning applications for major projects take decades to be considered. When matters are debated in the mother of parliaments, it often seems that the argument is dominated by partisan point scoring, laced with the occasional bit of special pleading on behalf of 'my constituents'. The only MPs who speak with genuine passion are the professional contras. You know who I mean.

Nowhere has this tendency been more pronounced than in relation to Europe. When a common market was first mooted, Britain was filled with disdain. Bunch of Frogs and Krauts and Eyeties, what do they know? We've got the British Commonwealth, and our good old buddies with the funny hats and check trousers. As it gradually dawns on us years later that a single market of hundreds of millions of consumers twenty-one miles of Channel away can't really be ignored, we apply late and sheepishly for membership. By now two things have happened. The agricultural policy, designed to support small French farmers and hugely disadvantageous to us, is set in concrete. And the bunch of foreigners who seemed keen to have our support in the 1950s have now gained in confidence, they're coping fine without us. When we do pluck up the courage to apply, the French tell us to bog off. What a triumph for British diplomacy. By the time we do join, we've missed the debate that shaped most of the major institutions of the Union.

Here's the bottom line. I'm a great admirer of our Prime Minister. He took a political party that was dead on its feet and turned it into an election-winning juggernaut. He's made us think seriously about all kinds of issues we've been ignoring for decades, such as welfare and work, competition and compassion, freedom and responsibility. But he, as much as any other contemporary leader, seems locked in the search for consensus, never daring to make a move unless the focus groups and the pollsters say it's OK. We need more leadership, less management. There is a powerful case for committing to join the Euro. There is a case, in my view less cogent, for staying out. There is no case for continuing to dither. Can you imagine Churchill in 1940 asking his staff for a focus group to help him decide whether to defend freedom and democracy? His heart told him what was right. Otherwise I wouldn't be writing these words. And you, my friend, wouldn't be reading them.

Be independent enough to be who you are, not part of the herd

It seems to me that each of us must identify in our personal history those who represented freedom in the world, those who managed to live just outside the rules, who seemed not beholden to the forces that held others in place. I am not thinking of literal criminal activity…but of someone who seemed to exude freedom by the way they lived, who was not a slave to all the truths repeated so easily by others, who had a breath of spontaneity in their lives.
David Whyte

On the ships the slaves were packed in the hold on galleries one above the other. Each was given only four or five feet in length and two or three feet in height, so that they could neither lie at full length nor sit upright. Contrary to the lies that have been spread so pertinaciously about Negro docility, the revolts at the port of embarkation and on board were incessant, so that the slaves had to be chained, right hand to right leg, left hand to left leg, and attached in rows to long iron bars. In this position they lived for the voyage, coming up once a day for exercise and to allow the sailors to 'clean the pails'. But when the cargo was rebellious or the weather bad, then they stayed below for weeks at a time. The close proximity of so many naked human beings, their bruised and festering flesh, the foetid air, the prevailing dysentery, the accumulation of filth, turned these holds into a hell. During the storms the hatches were battened down, and in the close and loathsome darkness they were hurled from one side to another by the heaving vessel, held in position by the chains on their bleeding flesh. No place on earth, observed one writer of the time, concentrated so much misery as the hold of a slave ship.

C.L.R. James, The Black Jacobins

You see, that's a real slave ship. That's real pain. That's real slavery. What you have to be clear on is whether you are your own worst slave trader. A slave trader in your head…

It's also important to remember that the conditions described in the extract above were the very conditions that helped to create Voodoo. The African slaves were determined to maintain some link not only to their homeland, but also to something that connected them to inspiration, passion and freedom. That was Voodoo. Out of pain and suffering was born the magic.

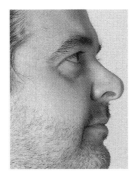

So, being free to choose, what would you like to work on?

EXERCISE

As we mentioned on page 9, we have a copy of *Time* magazine that says on the cover 'A Look Ahead.' And then there's the list of questions:

Will the recession end?
Can Bush stay popular?
Will there be a September 11 repeat?
Where's Bin Laden?
Is Arafat finished?
Can Chirac stay on top?
Will India and Pakistan nuke it out?
Will Schroder beat Stoiber?
Do I have to learn to tango?
Will oil stay cheap?
Will *The Lord of the Rings* top *Star Wars*?

Let's suppose the magazine is, in fact, named after you. So, Frank or Rebecca or whatever:

What are your 'Look Ahead' questions? We aren't interested here in life goal questions. We don't care what's going to be written on your gravestone. We don't care what sort of house you want to live in when you grow up. We're thinking of one year maximum – after that, who knows where you'll be?

So, with the next year in mind (the twelve months from whenever you're reading this), what do you want to ask about yourself and your life?

Do I have what it takes to get promotion?
Will I pass that exam?
Will I upgrade my car?
Can I keep in this relationship?
Will I be retained or laid off?
Will my friendships survive my getting married?

You get the picture.

What are the questions about your next year which are burning a hole in your midnight heart?

Now I'm going to ask you to write quickly and as far as possible without stopping. Don't take you eyes off the page in front of you. Try to connect the most truthful urgent questions from your soul to the pen, and don't let your critical mind get in the way. Ready?

So, what are the questions would you really like to engage with in this book?

Go!

IF YOU CAN'T WRITE THEM DOWN, THEY REALLY AREN'T QUESTIONS OF ANY SIGNIFICANCE, AND SO WILL BRING YOU NOTHING OF SIGNIFICANCE. FORGET ABOUT THEM.

NOW REVIEW THE ONES YOU HAVE WRITTEN DOWN.

CROSS OUT ALL BUT THREE. THAT MAY BE HARD, BUT DO IT ANYWAY.

THESE THREE QUESTIONS ARE THE ONES YOU'LL HAVE ANSWERS TO BY THE END OF THIS BOOK.

FOR THE PURPOSES OF WORKING THROUGH THIS BOOK, LET'S CALL THESE YOUR THREE VOODOO QUESTIONS.

WRITE THEM AGAIN HERE FOR CLARITY:
1.

2.

3.

Voodoo warns: who you are is your future...

TIME FOR REFLECTION

What has created these things, which you may call issues or problems or challenges, what has created the questions you want answers to, is the meeting of you and the world. Unless the world is reading this book, we can't work with it, so we'll have to make do with you. And so will you. The world won't change without you doing so first. Your issues, problems or challenges won't shift unless you shift first.

You have to be able to risk your identity for a bigger future than the present you are living.
Fernando Flores

So, *who* are you?

EXERCISE

What I add to the world by being alive is:

I have a passion for:

What I take from the world by being here is:

I react strongly against:

The atmosphere I help create in a group at work is usually:

How my past has most obviously moulded me in the present is:

How I piss people off or drag them down is:

The reason why I chose the Three Voodoo Questions is:

There are some big questions in there. Questions on whose answers hangs everything that follows in this book, and your life beyond this book…

I'd ask you to be open to going back to them when you have more time than today.

You know, when that great day comes when you have more time than today.

That great day when you put yourself, your identity and your purpose ahead of your excuses…

So we come to the end of the section entitled 'are you open?'

There should be a metric here, you know. There should be a self-test that will help you measure your Openness Quotient. A series of questions to which you answer A, B, C or D, where any A answer scores 3, any B answer scores 1 and so on, you know how they go.

But there isn't because you probably wouldn't fill it in, and because we can't think what good it would do you to know that your Openness Score was 78.

The best measure of your openness is in your responses to the exercises in this book, like the one above. And in particular, to two questions about all those questions…

EXERCISE: QUESTIONS ABOUT QUESTIONS

- ◆ How deeply did I go into thinking about these questions – or did I find myself, for whatever reason, telling myself I'd got the 'right' or 'good enough' answer straight away? The shallower the reflection, the less open you'll tend to be…

- ◆ What is the gap between how I responded and how I truly know I should have responded? The narrower the gap the more open you'll tend to be…

Voodoo asks:
'if you're
open,
what enters?

Voodoo: You too

From *Corporate Voodoo* to *My Voodoo*

In *Corporate Voodoo* we spoke fondly about Fast businesses, those role model Voodoo businesses that behaved in a manner that we felt very strongly identified with our mantra and beliefs. We explored four key areas, not just in terms of strategy but far more about the culture and emotions of the business, which were pivotal to understanding and delivering Voodoo. We called these the four ingredients of the Voodoo Spell:

◆ **Voodoo is risk embracing and courageous**
>> Not giving into to fear and uncertainty
>>> thinking BIG but acting small and agile; making bold decisions and dealing with the outcome, however it shows up

◆ **Voodoo loves virtual**
>> Not being weighed down by stuff
>>> not having to own or build the components of the business. Time to market and first prover are far more important

◆ **Voodoo is open-cultured**

Openness to recruiting talent from outside, even at senior levels

attraction of talent is seen as the key to their future. Loyalty is important, but contribution is vital

◆ **Voodoo is customer-led**

Close proximity to the customer

understanding the customer DNA, and believing that fundamentally all customers have (increasing) choice

We received some strong feedback after *Corporate Voodoo*. Not everyone agrees or buys into our view of how magic happens. In fact some people couldn't get past the word Voodoo. This frightened them off; perhaps they could not escape their pulls from the past. Quite a few of our readers felt that they were not able to do magic or that their issues were a little more close to home and they needed to sort those out first. This was the genesis of *My Voodoo*. My strong feeling was that the major thoughts and views expressed within *Corporate Voodoo* were just as applicable to individuals. More and more we all need and want to be the same person at home as at work, because guess what, we *are* the same person.

So here is the Voodoo Spell reconfigured for you the individual.

◆ **Voodoo is risk embracing and courageous** – Voodoo is bold and does not fear failure

There are times when we could all do with a dose of unadulterated courage. Those moments when we feel alone and empty. When the next step feels like stepping off the end of a very sheer and steep cliff. At these moments the Voodoo starts to play new rhythms with your heartbeats.

Don't be afraid to take a big step. You can't cross a chasm in two small jumps.
David Lloyd George

Take that big step. You may find it painful, but massively pleasing. You might just be good at big steps.

Courage is vital when endeavouring to understand who we are and how we behave; it may not all be good news, but it is essential to know. From this start point it becomes clear what we are comfortable with and proud of. It will also highlight the areas of discomfort, which we would like to change for the better.

To change and to change for the better are two different things.
German proverb

◆ **Voodoo loves virtual** – Voodoo values partnerships and friendships

He who knows others is wise.
He who knows himself is enlightened.
Lao Tzi (Tao Te Ching)

It is imperative to receive feedback and advice from the people who care about you and whom you respect. We spoke about the power of mentors, partners and friends in *Corporate Voodoo*. We now build upon these and explore the major benefits that access to caring relationships can deliver, especially during those moments of fear and disturbance. How often do you share your pain or your achievements?

The significant problems we face cannot be solved at the same level of thinking we were at when we created them.
Albert Einstein

◆ **Voodoo is open-cultured** – Voodoo embraces diversity

Do you have a diverse set of friends? Are you and all your main contacts similar? Do you all tend to do and think in the same manner? This may well be fine. However, you might just be missing out on some pretty meaningful and enjoyable stuff.

Character cannot be developed in ease and quiet. Only through experience of trial and suffering can the soul be strengthened, ambition inspired, and success achieved.
Helen Keller

We all live in an increasingly diverse world, and perhaps our world will never be the same again. Even though we all know that nostalgia gets better with time, this new world might just be all its cracked up to be. Take that risk; get involved. Embracing diversity is just so much better a feeling than living in fear of it.

◆ **Voodoo is customer-led** – Voodoo loves service

At times it is so easy to get totally engrossed in what we are doing. At times being quite oblivious to those who love and care for us. Raise our heads, make eye contact, be warm and reach out and touch. Never underestimate what a difference our attention and care can make to those around us. Go on, reach out and touch; it might just feel wonderful.

You must be the change you wish to see in the world.
Gandhi

We have met the enemy and it is us.
Walt Kelly, Pogo comic strip

This is the second of the Voodoo Volumes and we wrote this with you in mind.

THE TRUE SKELETON

There I sit trapped in my visible skeleton
One of bones, flesh, muscles and tissues
The false one. For most, the only one.
Yet, for me, there is another.
But in this one, the body and its complex workings
Act merely as a shell.

The true body being the mind,
And the soul being the imagination.
That is the true skeleton.

Becky Butler

Voodoo touches parts others cannot reach

I have always told my sons that they did not have my advantage of being born into abject poverty.
Kirk Douglas

Voodoo says: invest in yourself; renew yourself; revisit what you know

Voodoo is bold and does not fear failure

Voodoo values partnerships and friendships

Voodoo embraces diversity

Voodoo loves

Voodoo loves all of us

FIFTEEN PERSPECTIVES ON BRINGING MAGIC INTO YOUR LIFE AND WORK

So you've identified three burning questions which you'd like to focus on over the course of this book.

Now's the time to begin work on them.

We'd like to start by filtering your questions through the following ten lenses:

- ◆ CHANGE
- ◆ CHOICE
- ◆ SELF-RESPONSIBILITY
- ◆ INTEGRITY
- ◆ PERSONAL POWER

- ◆ POLITICAL POWER
- ◆ COURAGE
- ◆ IGNORANCE
- ◆ RESILIENCE
- ◆ KARMA

Whenever a problem is raised in a session we're running, it is usually illuminated and transformed by looking at it again from the perspective of one of these critical concepts.

We'll take each concept at a time, explain our take on it, and then let you reflect on what each concept has to tell you about your questions.

Here goes…

CHANGE

What is, is. What isn't, isn't.

If you're worrying about something that isn't you're wasting your heartbeats. Fears are a case in point. The something you are afraid of isn't, unless it is. Fear of drowning isn't real unless you're actually in some water.

If something is, *really* is, if a tiger is loose in front of you (for tiger read bankruptcy or cancer or finding that your partner has been unfaithful – or just read tiger), then what you must do is accept it as it is. You must embrace it as real, otherwise you may be tempted to do that other human thing: begin to pretend that the tiger isn't really there at all. You know, like my boy Ollie: "I have my hands over my eyes – you can't see me!" No, Ollie, get real.

So ignore what isn't – or what is outside the span of your influence, which amounts to pretty much the same thing – and accept what is. Then decide if you want what is to be different. And if you do, then make something happen, put your energy into addressing what needs to be done. Be a Magician and bring something into being, but only by focusing your energy where change can happen. Don't waste your heartbeats…

Get real, accept it, then change it if you want to, if it's yours to change. And leave behind what isn't yours to change.

That's all there is to know.

Apart from all the other stuff.

WHAT I NEED TO APPLY CONCERNING CHANGE TO MY THREE VOODOO QUESTIONS:

CHOICE

The trouble with you is not that you don't realise you have a choice in everything. You've read too much, you've been on too many courses, you're too smart to have failed to understand that whilst you can't control everything that happens to you, you can always control how you choose to respond. All those reactions, all that shouting and sulking and withdrawing and being angry and being positive and being persistent and being passionate and being grief-stricken at the death of a loved one, they're all choices you make to behave in a certain way. That's how powerful you are. None are natural by-products, none automatic consequences of events themselves. From all the multiplicity of human behaviour, you make a choice in how you respond to the event. The meaning is in you, not in the thing itself.

So you get that – even though in your laziest moments you'd prefer to believe that you're just a helpless victim, bobbing along like a cork in a storm praying to the great God of Pity.

You even get the idea that if you were able to press the pause button before you acted on your choice, and considered all the consequences, asking yourself 'Is this really in alignment with what I consider to be important and true?' – then you'd have fewer problems with putting short-term pleasure ahead of longer-term pain.

But none of that's your problem. Your problem is that too often you think that not choosing leaves you with lots of options open.

When in fact, not choosing leaves you in the shit. All doubt and confusion lives where you don't choose what to do about a situation.

Whereas taking action sets you free. Even the action which brings a painful consequence leaves you free to choose to respond to that consequence – and so things can unravel and progress. Not choosing is drowning in what isn't.

WHAT I NEED TO APPLY CONCERNING CHOICE TO MY THREE VOODOO QUESTIONS:

SELF-RESPONSIBILITY

We were walking from the car park to the Concert Hall and a bitter wind was blowing. As we walked quickly along the street, heads down against the chill, our friend – our host for the concert – said "Oh dear, I'm sorry it's so cold." "Excellent," said my wife Keri, "It's great that you're taking responsibility for the weather. Now I know who to blame!"

The only thing you can take responsibility for is yourself. The only thing you can easily change is yourself. You can't take responsibility for, or change, someone else's feelings or actions or beliefs any more than you can take responsibility for the weather, or for your cat.

People have to learn to take responsibility for how they respond to things, they have to take responsibility for what they think and what they feel. If I'm hurt because you tell me I'm a dreamer, that's my problem, not yours. I've got to learn what that hurt might be telling me.

This is not a moral principle, it's a Karmic one. It's not that we ought to take self-responsibility and if we do we'll go to Heaven. Rather it's that the results of our choices – what we say or do, or, equally, what we don't say or do – have inevitable consequences, both for us and others. And we need to face up to those consequences, because with freedom to choose comes responsibility.

What we choose to say and do, or not to say and do, affects the world, changes it in the moment, sends it in a new direction (or it might leave it continuing along the same path, of course, depending on what we said or did). If I ask you to close this book now and put it down, and you do, then both of us co-create that moment of 'stopping reading'. You could blame me for spoiling your evening, but you'd be wasting your heartbeats, because you chose to comply with my request. I need to take responsibility for the request I made of you. And you need to take responsibility for your compliance.

In this way, no matter what our level of political power in an organisation, we all help create our companies and can take some measure of responsibility for them.

And that means we can genuinely help talk or act them into change. We don't have to wait for our bosses, or the strategy document, or next month's sales meeting, or our customers. We can begin now, with us.

So too in our personal relationships. I don't have to wait for my kids to stop being naughty to be a good parent. My friend doesn't have to wait for his wife to stop being unfaithful to show her love. We can begin now, with us, to change what's ours to change, for the better.

WHAT I NEED TO APPLY CONCERNING SELF-RESPONSIBILITY TO MY THREE VOODOO QUESTIONS:

But you know about taking responsibility most of the time, don't you? Give your team an award and you'll be thrilled to let me know your contribution. But what about the other side of the coin? This is where we enter the realm of integrity.

The author Gary Zukav tells a wonderful story of a friend of his who is a frequent visitor to Italy. Out with his family for dinner, the bill arrives, and the friend's father, a fastidious man, checks every scribbled item as usual. After some study, he deciphers the last entry and finds it to be a short phrase which, roughly translated, means 'if it goes, it goes'. The father calls the head waiter and asks him what this means. The waiter shrugs. "It didn't go," he says.

How often for you does 'taking responsibility' feel more like the danger of being found out? Integrity holds no such fears.

Integrity is an alignment between what you value and your behaviour.

Integrity is also about facing up to the causes of the actions that produce negative consequences. Since our talk and action creates the reality we face, we need to take responsibility not only for what we want to change, but for what we have already created. The alcoholic cannot wish herself into being a non-drinker. The process is more rugged than that and a critical part of it is in owning up to those parts of us which are less than ideal. The 12 Step Programme starts with a confession, not a promise.

I like to hear a leader tell me how his passion, energy, discipline and sheer hard work are going to pull his company out of its doldrums. I'd be inspired if I heard him recognise the parts of him that helped contribute to the company as it currently is – in the doldrums. Everybody's got a plan, quite a few people are optimistic, but not enough are self-aware.

In a healthy organisation there is no conflict between what it says it is and what it actually is. Often, conflict arises from the difference between the espoused values on the Vision and Mission statement up on the reception wall, and the 'real' values that are lived out in the day to day reality. The conflict arises from the hypocrisy. It arises also from the difference between what a leader says she'll do and what she actually does.

The inevitability of being a hypocrite is that there is always something to hide.

Either you're hiding from what you said, from what you promised, from what you declared to the world about what would happen. Or you're hiding your 'true self' from the world, because you said one thing and, for whatever political reason, for whatever personal benefit, you need to live that promise out, even though what you promised was a deceit or a mistake ('My bosses told me to do it – I was just following orders').

Managers struggle with these issues day after day. The organisation makes a decision which you need to implement, even though it's against your principles or values. You make a promise to John that you'll do that much-postponed appraisal meeting with him this coming Friday – and then you're called by your own boss to an urgent strategy session. Your integrity is constantly being tested.

When you make a promise, the words you use have power, have reality, they are not just air, not just sound waves, they bring forth a world that is only there because you said those words. When your behaviour breaks a promise, that is an equally powerful act. It brings forth another world, a world in which what you say cannot be trusted.

Not walking your talk is a terribly stressful way to live, because at some level you're always scared you'll be found out. You'll be found out for being a fake, a con-artist, for not being up to the job. What fear! What tension! Think how much energy you're using to keep from being found out which you could be using for something much more positive and constructive.

Having integrity, on the other hand, is when there is nothing left to hide.

WHAT I NEED TO APPLY CONCERNING INTEGRITY TO MY THREE VOODOO QUESTIONS:

PERSONAL POWER

There's your personal power and the power you feel the need to exert because you've suddenly been given a team to lead. Or because you pay someone's National Insurance contributions.

Your personal power, they say, is a function of your self-belief, your confidence and your capacity for influencing the world around you. But all those things can be acted. They can be put on. And they usually are put on – noisily, and just prior to a walk over some burning coals. I don't know about you, but the most genuinely 'powerful' people I've met always seem to have a calm about them which is both reassuring and hugely attractive. There's no act. Their presence needs no forcing. And there is also a mystery about that calm which is compelling. I tell you what the big difference is: I always want to know more about them, rather than yearning to tell them all about what's going on for me…

Who do you know, or who have you seen, who is like that? And who do you know who is trying too hard to be 'charismatic'? What's the difference?

Six ways I'm aware of authentic personal power in others:

◆ When they can let things be as they are without the need to dominate

◆ When they are being for something rather than against something else[3]

---

[3] Mother Theresa was once asked by some protesters if she would join their March Against the Vietnam War. "No," she replied. "But when you hold a March for Peace, let me know."

◆ When they are listening for and demonstrating interest in others and the world

◆ When they are curbing the need to be right

◆ When they are giving rather than taking

◆ When they acknowledge and share their own inadequacies

Such power comes from the inside out.

WHAT I NEED TO APPLY CONCERNING PERSONAL POWER TO MY THREE VOODOO QUESTIONS:

POLITICAL POWER

Political power, on the other hand, is conferred on you by others; being promoted to manager is not an honour bestowed upon you, it's part of a bargain you enter into. You agree to be a certain way – and, in return, apart from getting a bit more money, you will be allowed to be that way. That's why there's so much trouble with managers. It's not because of a lack of training in managerial aptitude, nor because they are unaware of the softer skills termed Emotional Intelligence. It's because they're trying to be in a role that is not authentic to them and are being allowed to be that way – unchecked by us because we have followed our past conditioning and assumed that this is how bosses have to be. Management was originally a system designed to keep Roman slaves in check and we still haven't reinvented the concept or the practice.

But you don't need better theories about management, you need greater self-responsibility. All it takes is for you to be aware of how 'being a manager' shows up for you – and whether it moves you towards or away from what's needed.

What you require, then, is more awareness.

There are some major payoffs for being politically powerful: here are just five. How many of these strike a chord with your management of others?[4]

◆ Exercising control over others is a short cut to a belief which says 'you are separate from and better than others.' Built into all our conceptions of management is the belief that the manager is an improved version of what is below them.

[4] Whether it be at work, arranging the village fete or being a parent.

◆ Exercising control over others is a way to avoid your own insecurities. Being big in front of others means you never have to admit (to yourself or others) those times when you fail to make the grade.

◆ Exercising control over others keeps you busy (and goodness me, aren't we all so busy at the moment?) and therefore free from the distractions of quiet time, solitude and reflection.

◆ Exercising control over others guarantees you the recognition, acceptance and approval of others, even if it's faked, even if you don't deserve it, even if what you're being rewarded for doesn't align with your innermost values or principles

◆ Exercising control over others keeps you in the fantasy that there's a simple answer out there somewhere which, when found, will make everything work smoothly

I don't care what your business card says, how big your company is, what you are paid, how big you are. Whoever you are, if you're like the majority of us, you'll be human.

◆ You will never be separate, you'll always be just the same as others: *so make as much connection with your people as you can*

◆ You'll still be haunted by feelings of inadequacy: *so share your doubts, fears and mistakes*

◆ You'll find yourself, at some point, on your back in the dark staring up at the ceiling: *so consciously give yourself time for reflection and renewal*

◆ All the recognition, acceptance and approval of others you can engineer will not give you peace: *so exercise your integrity rather than your need to be liked*

◆ You'll always come back to the truth that life is difficult: *so try to accept the inevitable complexity, the struggles, the imperfection around you at work*

If you are a manager, do everything you can to step away from the hubris that is woven into the concept of being a boss.

If you are managed, and you want your manager to be better, try practising compassion rather than judgement, because that's more likely to draw them out of their instinct to dominate.

WHAT I NEED TO APPLY CONCERNING POLITICAL POWER TO MY THREE VOODOO QUESTIONS:

COURAGE

Courage is a much-overrated virtue, overrated because I think it is misunderstood. Ordinarily, it speaks of bravery and fearlessness, of extraordinary feats in the face of extraordinary odds.

Its imagery is to do with puffing up the chest, steeling the sinews, nerving oneself to the venture, shouting out loud, going 'Arrrgh!' as you run headlong into whatever you think is opposing you.

In all this imagery, there's something big and nasty out there which requires you to grow huge enough to combat it.

I'd propose different kinds of imagery.

The derivation of the word courage is a Latin noun 'cor', meaning 'heart'.

Courage is the act of behaving in alignment with what your heart says.

Behaving in alignment with what your heart says does not necessarily require there to be a big and nasty external enemy. It doesn't require a puffing out, it requires a turning in.

It may require a becoming big, but only if that's the size which your heart holds. If what your heart tells you matters enough to you, the challenge is aligning yourself with that.

This is what is happening, as just one example, when people tell us that they need courage to jump out of a steady career into the unpredictability of self-employment. The courage they need isn't actually in being brave enough to face a life of cashflow and self-motivation difficulties. The courage they need is in aligning themselves with what their heart is telling them is the right thing to do.

You can always overcome an external problem – there's always enough expertise out there to teach you how to Do Something. And there's always enough support to sustain you when you Fail.

The challenge is in doing it all anyway because in your heart you know it is inevitable…

WHAT I NEED TO APPLY CONCERNING COURAGE TO MY THREE VOODOO QUESTIONS:

IGNORANCE

Wisdom is the capacity for accepting how little you know.

What don't you know? How inadequate are you? What disables you?

After all that lifetime spent arming yourself with how clever and smart and sussed you are, how empty are you?

If you have emptiness, you are open to learning and growth, even if at this moment you don't know how that learning and growth will happen.

What do you know, now, that you don't know?

How vulnerable can you be in asking for help?

The known is finite, the unknown infinite; intellectually we stand on an islet in the midst of an illimitable ocean of inexplicability. Our business in every generation is to reclaim a little more land, to add something to the extent and solidity of our possessions.
Thomas Henry Huxley, On the Receipt of the Origin of Species (1887)

WHAT I NEED TO APPLY CONCERNING IGNORANCE TO MY THREE VOODOO QUESTIONS:

RESILIENCE

I'm blessed to have been able to work with individuals and groups across the planet. They've all had issues, problems, challenges. And they've all thought theirs were different, special, unique.

And that's because we all think we're all different, special, unique – and separate.

(A teacher of mine, Heather Campbell, used to say that the problems of the world were not in fact multifarious and numerous, but actually very limited in number and scope. I think she has a point. How about you?)

If I could carry with me a secret potion, one that I could get through the heightened security measures of the world's airports, it would be a potion that freed people from this great illusion, this great (dis)belief. Because we are all both different, special, unique and, at the same time, not at all different, special, unique. And we are certainly not separate (see Karma).

Dealing with the issues, problems and challenges of a single person or a huge group, requires two responses. One is that of the gentle friend, the empathiser: 'I'm sorry to hear how you feel, let me listen to and embrace your pain…' The other is that of the agent of change: 'Thanks for telling me how you feel; now, what are you going to do?'

So afraid are we of pain that there's a tendency to overdo the empathy. How often do you try to smother anger or upset when it happens by trying to heal it away?

The problem is that this overbalanced response reinforces another (dis)belief: that pain and upset is wrong. That when it turns up, we should do everything we can to subdue or even ignore it. Our emotionally-sanitised organisations are embodiments of this principle.

Of course pain and upset aren't wrong, it's just the way life is. And therefore what we need is resilience to work through it.

I've learnt all this again, just this year, in being around my two small boys. I've been able to pinpoint the awakening of the realisation that life is difficult and that resilience is what you need when you can't get all your own way. Ask Sam. He's four.

He will be able to tell you now that sometimes in life you simply do not get all your own way. And no amount of tantrums or tears will alter that.

WHAT I NEED TO APPLY CONCERNING RESILIENCE TO MY THREE VOODOO QUESTIONS:

KARMA

I took my dog out for a walk one summer evening. He's a big dog, so what actually happened was that he dragged me for a trot, but anyway you get the picture. Beautiful evening, light mottling through the trees, big blue open sky, fresh, fresh, air. God is in His Heaven and all's right with the world.

We came to the entrance of the field Chester usually runs in – you know the one, looking down over the valley to the east – only to find that the farmer had populated the field with sheep. And he'd ringed off a substantial part of the field with an electric fence, leaving a six-foot-wide channel at the edge where the public footpath runs.

So Chester goes bounding along the footpath stopping every so often to sniff gingerly at the electric ribbon and the sparse clumps of darkened wool that it held. And I'm thinking: I wonder what effect an electric fence has on a big dog like Chester?

Chester will not go near that field any more. He has learned that actions have consesquences. He's a smart dog.

How about you?

Not one day in anyone's life is an uneventful day, no day without profound meaning, no matter how dull and boring it might seem, no matter whether you are a seamstress or a queen, a shoeshine boy or a movie star, a renowned philosopher or a Down's-syndrome child. Because in every day of your life, there are opportunities to perform little kindnesses for others, both by conscious acts of will and unconscious example. Each smallest act of kindness – even just words of hope when they are needed, the remembrance of a birthday, a compliment that engenders a smile – reverberates across great distances and spans of time, affecting lives unknown to the one whose generous spirit was the source of this good echo, because kindness is passed on and grows each time it's passed, until a simple courtesy becomes an act of selfless courage years later and far away. Likewise, each small meanness, each thoughtless expression of hatred, each envious and bitter act, regardless of how petty, can inspire others, and is therefore the seed that ultimately produces evil fruit, poisoning people whom you have never met and never will. All human lives are so profoundly and intricately entwined – those dead, those living, those generations yet to come – that the fate of all is the fate of each, and the hope of humanity rests in every heart and in every pair of hands. Therefore, after every failure, we are obliged to strive again for success, and when faced with the end of one thing, we must build something new and better in the ashes, just as from pain and grief, we must weave hope, for each of us is a thread critical to the strength – to the very survival of the human tapestry. Every hour in every life contains such often-unrecognized potential to affect the world that the great days for which we, in our dissatisfaction, so often yearn are already with us; all great days and thrilling possibilities are combined always in this momentous day.

Dean Koontz, From the Corner of His Eye (Reverend Harrison White)

WHAT I NEED TO APPLY CONCERNING KARMA TO MY THREE VOODOO QUESTIONS:

Voodoo asks: are you finally going to turn over the closed sign?

We're our own dragons as well as our own heroes,
and we have to rescue ourselves from ourselves.
Tom Robbins

Voodoo says:
Lift the Curse

We hope that if you've reflected on each of the ten aspects, you'll have gained some significant insights into your three questions:

◆ some new ways of thinking about your issues

◆ something you need to do

◆ something you have to do differently

◆ something you've got to make happen

◆ something you have to complete

◆ a decision you have to make

◆ a conversation you need to have.

We hope, too, that you are feeling more clear about your issues, a little more energised, a little more confident.

We hope you want to do something about your issues.

But first, we ask you to pause and reflect on what might stop you making the magic happen.

We'd like to spend a little time examining five barriers to change we've witnessed in human beings over the world. When faced with a problem people are usually, with a bit of coaching, pretty good at coming up with solutions. And they are usually pretty motivated to want to do something about them.

And then they find they didn't look at themselves first, they didn't look at these five personal barriers, 'dragons' as Tom Robbins refers to them, which, if left to run loose, will burn down your hopes and dreams for change.

In the pages that follow, we've given you a provocation about each of the five dragons and asked you to complete two simple statements.

Go!

SELF-PITY

The 'Poor Me' in you is a defence against you growing up and taking responsibility...

What you know about yourself and Self-pity, particularly with reference to your Three Voodoo Questions is:

What you need to do to diminish its impact:

BLAME

Whereeever we feel powerless, there's where we're most ready to blame…

What you know about yourself and Blame, particularly with reference to your Three Voodoo Questions is:

What you need to do to diminish its impact:

WORRY/STRESS

Whenever you have conversations with yourself about lack or shortages or incompleteness, that's when stress rises up…

What you know about yourself and Worry/Stress, particularly with reference to your Three Voodoo Questions is:

What you need to do to diminish its impact:

APATHY/CYNICISM

Our cynicism is not an expression of disappointment with others and their actions, but a barely acknowledged intimation that we are the ones who will have to take responsibility if we want our world to be better – and it is that which makes us angry, bitter and scared…

What you know about yourself and Apathy/Cynicism, particularly with reference to your Three Voodoo Questions is:

What you need to do to diminish its impact:

PROCRASTINATION

Not now, but tomorrow. Not this year, but surely next. Procrastination is not a gathering of energies for some future big push; rather it drains both time and energy, since it adds self-doubt to self-delusion.

What you know about yourself and Procrastination, particularly with reference to your Three Voodoo Questions is:

What you need to do to diminish its impact:

How did it feel to have these issues raised about your character? It's one thing to be inspired towards the light, it's another to become comfortable with examining our darker aspects. But they exist and are as real and as full of learning as anything we experience.

Self-pity, apathy and the like are not wrong, in any moral sense. But the five dragons we've looked at here are unlikely to produce anything meaningful or magical in your life. Part of you will aspire to fly, another part will try to drag you down by the heels.

Indeed, the more you try to change, the more you'll become aware of the five dragons attempting to stop you. They will also rise up whenever you meet problems, mistakes or hazards as you work on your Three Voodoo Questions.

So let's do a quick exercise on this. The more awareness you have now, the stronger you'll be when upsets arise.

EXERCISE

When something goes wrong – when something unpleasant and unpredictable has turned up, when you've made a mistake, when your integrity's been blown, when your courage has gone, when you've been found out as inadequate – how do you respond?

Make excuses?
Get defensive/offensive?
Sulk/withdraw?
Use other avoidance tactics?
Lie?
Drink?
How could you respond?

1.

2.

3.

4.

5.

*Voodoo brings
it all together*

STOP!

Are those Three Voodoo Questions you wrote down   1.
earlier in the book the ones you really should be
concerned about?   2.

What do you think?
                                                        3.

Is it time to change them?

What's really burning in you to be answered?

For each of your Three Voodoo Questions, write down three conclusions you've made about the problem, and then three commitments you'll make (to yourself or to others) to bring change to that issue.

VOODOO QUESTION ONE:

Three conclusions I've reached

Three commitments I'm making

VOODOO QUESTION TWO:

Three conclusions I've reached

Three commitments I'm making

VOODOO QUESTION THREE:

Three conclusions I've reached

Three commitments I'm making

If you are still not sure, in the next section of *My Voodoo* you'll be able to listen to some other points of view…

This book is about opening up – to yourself, to others, to your dreams, to your current behaviours and attitudes.

The natural consequence of opening up is that at some point you'll be connecting to other human beings. And rather than seeing how different they are from you, you'll find in the end that connecting to other human beings is a little like looking in the mirror. Their fears and habits will be reflections or refractions of yours, as will their hopes and strivings. Through their issues, you'll re-engage with your own; through their decisions, you'll be re-inspired.

The Maverick Q+A

Any organisation, any community, any world has its fair quota of mavericks and fools, deviants and square pegs, agents of change, call them what you will. People who are passionate about the future, people who feel constrained by the status quo, people who can't believe that their leaders are behaving in the way that they are.

Doing the sort of work I do, and writing the sort of books I do, a good number of these mavericks have contacted me over the years. I'm always surprised that there are more people who think like this than we might, in our loneliest moments, suspect. We are not alone.

I remember doing a 'Fool's Clinic' once at a big conference. People could book half an hour of my time and get an objective, straight from the heart and the gut, chunk of feedback about their particular 'issue'. About a third of the people had brought, as briefed, a problem. Another third came along because they were intrigued by the title of 'Fool's Clinic' and wanted to know what I was on about. The remaining third came along to say "I'm the Fool in my company – let me tell you how it is!" They wanted to know where the Fool Collective was…

The one thing I believe to be true about these mavericks is that they can't help it. They didn't choose this way of thinking. It's how they are.

And given that the world is not, by definition, maverick, the crashing together of the two cultures (maverick and non-maverick) is sometimes a hard one, often a frustrating one.

But from frustration springs learning, if you let it. So, in that spirit, here are a few of the things that people have asked me over the years about the challenges they face in being as they are in the face of apparent cynicism, frustration, and hostility.

All of these are genuine cases sent by email – but I've removed names and other details, since these people never dreamt they'd be appearing in a book.

EMAIL 1

QUESTION

David! Is corporate culture in the UK/USA really changing overall?

I'm reading more and more articles about work/life balance, innovation and involving the entire firm in change. But I still see colleagues work ridiculous hours and be alienated from their work.

ANSWER

Wooooo, complex issue. One part of this is that thinking changes ahead of action, so that we can consider Good Things like wellbeing and co-created change long ahead of actually being able to do much about them. But there are real things happening, wonderful successes to celebrate in some organisations. It'll take a lot of time for these newer approaches to reach critical mass. And in a way, does it matter if they never do? We all do the best we can.

Also, the past has a huge pull on us, so that humans continue to recreate the past rather than embrace the future. The past is safe and trustworthy. The other thing is the dependency issue: people would rather do what they think of as suffering rather than take responsibility for doing something radical about it. Could be that people actualy like it as it is? Working ridiculous hours is an affirmation for some of their value in the world, and being alienated from their work/company is a tremendous way to socialise: 'Every other bugger is complaining so why not join the group?' Just how intense is this pain and alienation, in any case? You say you work in a big five accountancy company, surrounded by moderately wealthy people. Just how easy do they expect life to be?

In my workshops, I have less and less patience with people who tell me how shit their company is but still bank the salary every month.

Final point is that the way things are – fast – is exactly what we asked for. Speed was the mantra through the nineties and now we've got it, but perhaps not in the way we anticipated. It's a bit rude of us now to ask the universe for peace and happiness as well as speed. We should have thought of that earlier.

And the result of working in such a world is overload, exhaustion, etc. It just goes with the territory. So for example I like to think I'm someone who is following my dream, being passionate and creative, empowered and having fun at work – and at the same time, I struggle every week with disjointedness, doubt, pressure and work/life balance. Life is difficult.

Final final point is one I've got more clearly since writing the book: you can only ever work where you're working, can only ever influence what you can influence, can only ever take care for yourself and the people in front of/around you. What the rest of the world is up to doesn't matter. What moves/speaks to this client, what is possible here now, today, that's what matters. And when we've got clarity and commitment on that, then we'll expand their influence to those wider matters.

Similarly, never mind whether 'corporate culture in the world' is changing – what matters is whether the experience of work is changing for you. If not, what can you do?

EMAIL 2

QUESTION
My colleagues are all scared of me – being honest that is. Sometimes no amount of padding can cushion the blow of what you are really saying. I'm seen as a maverick with no right to be such... 28, girl, been in job 7 months, who is expected to be that bit more grey, that bit less irreverent... what do I do to ensure that my way can be accepted here? I don't say anything unless I truly believe it to be utterly right... I'm not spouting off willy-nilly.

ANSWER
I'd guess this is a pretty accurate summary of the way it is. If you are doing what you say, then the probability is that they are behaving in that way because you're upsetting their expectations of you.

Work is pressurised enough without you sticking your oar in. But you're not going to stop sticking your oar in, so...

You ask '... what do I do to ensure that my way can be accepted here?' Consider this: it may never be accepted. People will focus on your personality rather than your message. Inevitable. And besides, they expect you to be quiet rather than troubling, you expect them to be comfortable with your honesty. Who should have their way?

If it won't be accepted, go for effectiveness. Don't just tell them what, but why. To what end are you telling this truth? What greater good is it meant to move the company to (as opposed to the short term and perceivedly selfish buzz it gives you to say what's on your mind)?

And do more of that 'why' explaining after the event, when the heat of upset has died down. Show that you are reflective and thoughtful about what you say, and that it fits into a wider context that would be meaningful to the person or persons concerned...

EMAIL 3

QUESTION

I want to sell the idea of corporate change to my company which is still working in the 70s mindset (hierarchy, ethos, us & them) etc. What's the best way to get the managers to buy it? (I've already broached it once & got told 'it isn't the right time, all sorts of things are happening behind the scenes', etc... in other words 'go away & play little girl'. This was 6 months ago and we're in a worse mess now than then.

ANSWER

1. Choose your battles wisely. Don't go banging your head against the brick-wall managers – find the people in the organisation (at any level) who would be most open to what you mean and talk with them about the possibility of change.

2. Clarify what you mean by corporate change. That's a huge, unhelpful, scary phrase likely to have

people running back to the status quo. What specifically are the organisation's problems? What do you have – or can you acquire – that will help the organisation solve those problems? If your company is really in a 70s mindset, then it will like to solve problems. Solving problems is easier than 'change'.

3. You say
'I've already broached it once & got told "it isn't the right time, all sorts of things are happening behind the scenes," etc... in other words "go away and play little girl."'

As a change agent, you'll need to handle rejection better than that. How do you know what they meant? Did God create you a mindreader? They're probably telling you the truth as they see it in any case – there probably are 'all sorts of things…happening behind the scenes' which are more urgent than corporate change. Get curious. Step into their shoes – how do they see the world and its challenges – and how can you shape your offering to that?

EMAIL 4

QUESTION
Hi David! How can I turn my maverick habits of a life time into money? I know I see things very differently to other (normal) people. I'm 48 years old and can't take any more of this abuse…Please help if you can!

ANSWER
Why would you want to turn them into money?

Why not turn them into art?

Seriously, what do you turn them into now? Does the abuse come from the maverick habits or from the normalcy around you? Either way, charging money won't free you from the abuse (I know).

EMAIL 5

QUESTION

After working in a company for 4-plus years I am now going freelance partly because I feel my ideas and the way I think are not appreciated or understood by the company. Now I feel sad. I would like to work within a group that I felt I belonged to (and in whose aim I believed in) and that I felt valued my mind. While freelancing does seem a more attractive prospect than where I am now, I think I partly feel sad because I haven't fitted in and wonder if this is ever possible to do so, as a maverick, in the corporate world. How do I (I am happy to call myself a maverick) fit in if I am by nature an outsider? Do all mavericks fear financial insecurity because of their outsider nature? What do you suggest I do with this feeling that I have to normalise myself?

ANSWER

There's a lot in your question. I'd like to challenge a couple of assumptions:

1. 'not being appreciated or understood' by the company is not necessarily a sign that you are an outsider.
2. what does 'outsider' mean for you? How do you know you are one?
3. what would 'fitting in' look like? Why do you want it?
4. how could you 'be a maverick' and 'fit in'?
5. as for the feeling to normalise yourself (and what does that mean?), either act on it, or accept it for what it is: just a feeling.
6. the money thing is nothing to do with being a maverick or an outsider. It's just a money thing. I know quite a few 'insiders' who fear financial insecurity.

Hope that sets you thinking for a while.

EMAIL 6

QUESTION
Why won't my company change? It's horrible here. But I have a family and a mortgage to pay for. It's all right you saying 'think for yourselves' and 'be free'. It's different for me.

ANSWER
You're right. You're exempt. You're different. What you are experiencing has never been experienced by anyone ever before.

Stay where you are. You'll get used to the pain. Besides, you may have only 38 years left to live, and only 16 of those with the company…

EXERCISE

'Preparedness' must replace fear because we cannot expect much advance information about what new situation might happen next.

The path becomes the "key" and not the destination, as the latter itself changes.

'Implementability' becomes more important than the right solution.
www.nonlinearthinking.com

DISCUSS, WITH REFERENCE TO PERSONAL EXPERIENCE AND FEELINGS
(10pts)

Voodoo People: How it really is out there

Ideas and insights from six readers of *Corporate Voodoo*...

Some people buy books.

Some people read the books they buy.

Some people are just pleased to own the books.

Some people read the books they buy all the way through.

Some people feel moved, in whatever way, by the books they read all the way through.

Some people feel so moved, in whatever way, by the books they read all the way through that they contact the authors.

And sometimes what those people say makes the authors of those books so very aware that they are still learning, still listening, still amazed at what real people are facing in their real lives every day.

So we asked a few of the people who contacted us to write something about how they felt, something about how they saw the world in these strange times. Something about how coming in to contact with the Voodoo vision had affected them.
Here are their stories...

CARL BAINBRIDGE
Creating Personal Voodoo – Breaking the Status Quo

Before Voodoo

I had always been successful at my work, making my way in the IT industry through various project management, marketing and sales roles. I had always met targets, even won various sales prizes but always found it tough, always felt I was working harder than I needed to – never quite believing it was me. I was continually asking myself what else I could do but never really came up with any compelling answers. Therefore I just kept ploughing on – keeping the status quo. This was a pattern I was familiar with. I had always drifted through life without making the major decisions. I chose my A-levels because everyone else did them. I chose my degree because it left my options open and I chose my job because there was a long queue at the careers fair and they were offering the chance to get into computers which seemed a good idea at the time. When accepting subsequent jobs, I was always moving away from something as opposed to towards any deep-rooted calling. This pattern was similar to other aspects of my life – even relationships. I had drifted along in far too many without being able to take the next step. 'Get a life,' I hear you say!

Creating my Voodoo

Things changed about 2 years ago. I had found myself in a job as an IT consultant in a leading management consultancy that I had little passion for. It looked good (to others and on the CV) but felt wrong! Typical! I had just heard my practice head claiming that all his troops had a passion for building IT systems and something jarred with me. My stomach tightened. I knew that I didn't have any such passion (Lesson 1: listen to those gut reactions –

understand what is causing them and do not bury them). Around that time my partner had become seriously ill and it challenged my priorities. I therefore took 6 months off work – clearly to be with her, but also to get a break from the rat race. To clear my mind and think!

During this time, I gained some interesting insights into what I had liked and disliked about various jobs and projects. I began to realise that practically all the times I had got any real buzz from work had been when I was training or coaching other people. I started noticing what excited me in the various magazines I read, which articles got the adrenaline going. They were all around learning, getting people to break out of their comfort zones, people who were creating and following a passion (Lesson 2: notice what articles grab your attention – read more of them). So when I was offered the chance (by my very understanding company) to come back into their change management practice, I jumped at it. It was different. I was nervous about not really having much expertise in this area. But I went for it. By staying in the same company, at least I was preserving a degree of familiarity (stretching the comfort zone as opposed to marching into the panic zone!). However, it didn't turn out to be what I had hoped for. Substitute the words change management for IT and there was the same flatness. Still no passion. No soul. I got pretty low. I started doubting myself. Perhaps it was just me. Perhaps I was just not up to it. Perhaps my whole approach to work was wrong? I was on the point of quitting as it had started to affect my home life – the absolutely last thing that my partner needed as she was making a courageous and brave fightback from her illness. That I could be so self-centred when she was so amazingly strong…

Then, having finished one particularly uninspiring assignment about a year ago, I found myself with some time and I put myself on a couple of training courses. Anything to take the pressure off. One of these was 'Train the Trainer' and its impact was startling. I could never have imagined it beforehand, but I loved it. I felt at ease, I excelled, offered opinions, gave great feedback, felt inspired. All this from a simple course. I was then offered the chance to deliver the programme – and rather nervously accepted. It went down a storm – the reviews were great and I felt like I had arrived. One particular participant who I had coached through what was a particularly difficult experience said it had transformed her whole working life. How rewarding was that!

This all fuelled my interest in what makes people learn and what makes them change. I was amazed by the dryness of all the corporate approaches to change management with all their frameworks and models. I read more and more books and articles on this stuff. I'm OK, You're OK and The 7 Habits of Successful People became my bibles (pre-Voodoo, you understand). I took afternoons off and sat in my local coffee shop for hours on end (Lesson 3: do more of what you enjoy and less of what you don't). It became my sanctuary – the sofas, the ambient music and general hubbub enabled me to create some space where I could just lose myself in my interest. Ideas and energy flowed. It was where I did my contemplating (Lesson 4: create your own space – you do not find your Voodoo by telling yourself to think when you got a spare 5 minutes). I was more fun to be around at home, I was engaging more fully with my partner, my friends and family. Life was now going on outside my own head. It was weird – life just seemed simpler (Lesson 5: when the voodoo comes it comes in leaps and bounds – ride the wave). I could never have anticipated the effect on all aspects of my life.

Since this time I have run more and more client development workshops and coaching sessions. I read about new ideas and concepts and they slot right into programmes I am designing. It feels like I have been doing this for years. I have so much energy. I never thought I would truly believe it, but I do look upon errors and mistakes as learning opportunities. I am confident enough for them not to threaten me. I know I am good, so I do not waste time worrying so intently about what others think. I just try things and if they work, great; if they do not, then OK too.

Reading the book

And this brings me to *Corporate Voodoo*. I read it and was struck by the emphasis you placed on the personal aspects. Creating Voodoo is not easy. The temptation to maintain the status quo was for me overwhelming and had been for many years, despite the fact that that kind of life just didn't seem to be what I wanted. The hard part was that you don't miss what you have never had. I didn't realise how uplifting and rewarding my work could be so I could never get in touch with what that could be like. My only frame of reference was what had gone before and these limiting beliefs are hard to overcome. One thing that really helped was finding myself someone to talk to – a coach if you like. Someone who could understand and empathise. Someone to act as that sounding board. Someone who, when I got a glimpse of what life could be like, was there to help push me over the edge and go for it (Lesson 6: find a good sounding board – pay if you need to; it is the wisest money you could spend).

Your book and others like it can act as a catalyst but when you are as stuck as I was, perhaps even this is not enough to create real and lasting change. The extra impetus I received from my coach was vital and it is this combination of spark/catalyst and support/coaching that I think was critical to me creating my own personal Voodoo. No-one can do it except you but sometimes a helping hand is vital.

Carl is a consultant in a leading management consultancy

CARL BAINBRIDGE
A Reflection

Sometimes it takes a major event to give us perspective and the will to change.
I am constantly reminded that there are always those around us who can give so much and never give up. This must serve to encourage and inspire, if only we can see, hear and feel their communication with us. It is not always verbal; it is sometimes delivered by deed or by hush. When the Voodoo is happening do we have the necessary Voodoo antennae?

The longer we run in the same race with the same contestants, to the same rules, we must and will improve, and that is a very common story sold us by our teachers, our bosses, our leaders. Carl found himself improving and doing OK, but not feeling OK. And maybe that's the deal; perhaps that's what we sign up to. But is it going to be enough? Is this present the future you want?

We have just read that the future can be seriously and compellingly different. We were left with some very personal Voodoo lessons. I resonated with all of them:

Lesson 1: listen to those gut reactions – understand what is causing them and do not bury them
Anxiety, excitement, stress or ecstasy all cause a gut and physical reaction – understand them. When we feel really good and positive it is vital to understand the best way of making the feeling last or at least learn how to repeat it. The only way is to understand what caused it.

What made me feel like that? What's the pattern? This is important. This is Voodoo.

Nothing great was ever achieved without enthusiasm.
Ralph Waldo Emerson

Lesson 2: notice which articles grab your attention – read more of them

Examine what you regularly read or listen to and ask yourself how you felt having read it. Identify the stuff that makes you feel positive and inspired. See if there is a particular magazine, newspaper, website, book, or TV/radio programme that is closest to how you want to live and who you want to be. Make the effort to engage with it frequently. Some of my best friends are books.

The ultimate measure of a man is not where he stands in moments of comfort, but where he stands at times of challenge and controversy.
Martin Luther King

Lesson 3: do more of what you enjoy and less of what you don't

Never underestimate how much choice we have. Always question routine. Humans are great creatures of habit. We have developed these immune systems which switch off our ability to challenge the boringly repetitive and easily changed. Some of these activities may have been in place for years, unchallenged and no longer thought about. Travelling exactly the same route in the same transport, shopping at the same stores, eating the same food, working in the same company, living the same life.

112 / MY VOODOO

He who joyfully marches in rank and file has already earned my contempt. He has been given a large brain by mistake, since for him the spinal cord would suffice.
Albert Einstein

Lesson 4: create your own space – you do not find your Voodoo by telling yourself to think when you've got a spare 5 minutes

The more we plan, the more we deliver. It is increasingly easy and normal to spend our lives being busy. If we do not plan for our holidays, they rarely happen as we would want them to. Use the same approach for your time and space. We all need to make the time to think about how we could be happier. This needs quality Voodoo time. Take that time to travel to your very own Voodoo space and place, at your pace.

Lesson 5: when the voodoo comes it comes in leaps and bounds – ride the wave

That good old *Corporate Voodoo* temporary monopoly. When everything is in your gift. The Midas touch. When it happens, it will not last forever. Capitalise and exploit upon the experience whilst you can, but do have plan B ready for when the music stops playing.

Live as if you were to die tomorrow. Learn as if you were to live forever.
Gandhi

When drinking from the fountain of youth, do not make the mistake of sipping or feeling a little full; you may never come this way again.

Lesson 6: find a good sounding board – pay if you need to; it is the wisest money you could spend

We agree. In *Corporate Voodoo* we spoke about a mentor being a sorcerer for magic…and there's more on mentoring on page 193-199.

Our character is what we do when we think no one is looking.
H. Jackson Browne

CHRIS CORBIN
Shallow Reefs

I turned 46 last week and what do I most want to do? Surf – the ocean and its waves; that's my voodoo. Is it because I'm in a mid-life crisis? I don't think so, I went through that a few years ago. It is because I have surfed all my life and as I get older I become more aware of how much I've learned from surfing.

Why do I love surfing? There are a host of reasons; one is that I like being scared. To become even moderately competent as a surfer you have to spend time being scared. Sooner or later the day comes when you find yourself out in waves that are bigger than they looked when you decided to paddle out and you have to make a choice, 'Do I turn tail and paddle back in (and endure the ridicule of your fellow surfers) or do I swallow hard and have a go?' Your experience to date tells you that if you can conquer your fear and ride even one of these great beasts you will experience a thrill like no other and you will become an expanded person in the process. You decide to go for it.

Voodoo disrupts routine

Voodoo encourages you to think about you

Voodoo cups
never runneth
over

YOUR REFLECTION ON THIS STORY

On the first wave you get to your feet and look down into a chasm that seems higher than a house – have you ever been doing repairs to the roof of your house, crept to the edge and looked over? It's the same feeling. Through the clear water you can see the sharp edges of the reef and you know that if you get this wrong you could be badly hurt, maybe even killed, but it's too late now; there's no going back. You manage to get past that moment, keep control and make the wave. You're through it. 'Whoaaah!' The feeling is way better than you imagined. The later waves you catch are much less scary, your confidence builds and even when you wipeout it's not as bad as you expected. You survive the session with aching limbs and a graze on your shoulder.

How competent you become is in direct proportion to the level of fear you encounter. A world class surfer who later became several times world surf champion tells the story of the first time he paddled out on a big day at Pipeline (a renowned break on the Hawaiian island of Oahu that breaks in 3 to 4 feet of water over a jagged coral reef) – and defecated in his board shorts! And what about the guys who now regularly surf 30 to 40 foot waves breaking on off-shore reefs at places with names like Jaws and Mavericks? What kind of fear thresholds have they survived?

A week before my 46th birthday I was surfing a 6-8 foot reef break in the Caribbean – was I scared? No: I'd paid my dues; done my fear – I was challenged and happy. The same day another group of surfers were surfing on the same coast but on a much shallower reef and several of them got badly cut. Do I wish I had been there? No, by virtue of being a bit older, I'm a bit wiser so I have no desire (or maybe only a faint and illusory desire) to ride Jaws on a 40-foot day. I've listened to my voodoo.

How does my voodoo inform my work? Well, I have faced some fears, I've looked down and 'seen the reef' but I survived with only a grazed shoulder. So now I can turn up at a client assignment, draw on my experience and expertise and almost always have a good ride. When I do 'wipeout' it serves to remind me of things I had forgotten and I'm better placed for the next piece of work.

So what are my 'shallow reefs'; my 'Jaws' and 'Mavericks'? I am challenged and happy when I am dealing with issues between and about people; I'm scared when the CEO of a global business wants to debate with me the intricate details of a financial re-structuring, his strategy for penetrating a new market or the re-alignment of his global strategic positioning. I can't hear anything about people; now I'm scared – and my voodoo tells me I should be!

Chris Corbin grew up in Barbados; married, father of 3 and still surfing,
Chris now lives in England and works with Potential Partnership and Telos Partners.
Chris.Corbin@PotentialPartnership.com

CHRIS CORBIN
A Reflection

There are three things that resonate with me about Chris's piece.

The first is the passion with which he talks about his surfing and its impact. You can tell the essence of surfing is in his whole being, his head, his heart, his body (grazed shoulder and all). There's a reminder there for all would-be Voodoo Initiates; whatever you do, do it with enthusiasm. Wherever you are, look for what touches you, moves you, inspires you. How long have you been married? Look for seven things in your partner NOW that keep you in love with him or her. How long have you been in your job? Find something NOW that touches you, moves you, inspires you about it. Think that your job is a meaningless cog in someone else's big wheel? Then find the reason NOW that your world – your circle of influence, your colleagues, your boss, your friends and family directly affected by your morale in this job – will be improved by the work you'll do tomorrow.

What's your passion?

The second resonance in Chris's piece is the attitude to fear. Fear comes – inevitably, obviously, sanely, naturally – and then it passes. You anticipate it, plan for it, get scared by it, it happens – and then you find yourself on the other side…That's true of all aspects of life, not just on the water. Fear does not disable the life-surfer. The life-surfer disables the life-surfer, if that's what they choose…

And that's connected to my third insight from Chris's piece. Not this time, the attitude to fear, but the attitude to the wave.

'…you get to your feet and look down into a chasm that seems higher than a house…'

You don't have to be on a surfboard to experience this. Sometimes you can be standing on a station platform, you can be halfway through a conversation with your partner, you can be lying on your back in the dark staring up at the ceiling, when the abyss opens up. That moment when you question everything, when you doubt even yourself.

It doesn't matter how old you are or how young. If you're three years away from retirement, maybe you suddenly realise you're facing the awful waste that you've called your career. Just at the moment you get exactly what you want – all that freedom that you could never grant yourself in the company, which you'll now claim to have on the golf course and the cruise ship or in the bar every day at five to opening time. And just at that moment you get to realise how you've chosen to spend those two-and-a-half billion heartbeats.

If you're young and single, maybe you suddenly face up to the end of cynicism, that warm mother-pap of ironic detachment, and you begin to see that cynicism too, even that, is pointless and won't sustain you.

If you're somewhere in between, maybe you look again at that face your partner gives you every night when you come home and realise it is saying 'what are you doing with your life…?'

If you're a successful careerist, working your way up the ladder to a life of reserved car spaces at the office and interior designers at home, maybe you find yourself not being able to say no to the CEO when the answer is yes, or yes when the answer is no, and in that moment your identity, your integrity, seems to crumble.

This is the abyss.

And then there is the other side of the abyss, and flesh grazed on the sharp rocks as the consequence. But the abyss opens up as inevitably and naturally as fear, and you must find reserves, or help, to learn, adapt and move through. To wish away the abyss in our lives is like trying to wish away the waves in the ocean.

Chris Corbin asks: "What will this wave give me?" We must ask: "What is the abyss asking us to look at?"

YOUR REFLECTION ON THIS STORY

MORGAINE GAYE
Falling

It was a typically hot September morning and I stood at my window watching thousands of suited and booted men and women running down the West Side Highway. A far as I could see, there was a sea of people moving off into the distance. I stepped outside and the air was thick and white. Sunlight was barely visible. Small desk trinkets and personal photos fell from the sky. Melted CDs and half-burned documents littered the roads. The personal world that each person had created around their desk was gone. Family pictures, little plastic things which came from somewhere or other, post-it notes with memos and numbers on them, some snacks in the second draw down, lip balm, hand cream, spare tie (essential, but never used), office supplies in a desk tidy, laptop, mobile phone – all these things were erased. The office landscape was destroyed.

So what remained of the corporate world for people whose job was a chore; for people who spent hours a day on the internet in search of a distraction; for those people who created a secure home-from-home handbag existence by surrounding their desks with trivia? It was a drastic wake-up call for so many who decided that the world to which they had so tightly clung had no meaning and was not integral to the happiness and fulfilment they desired.

'Life is too short' became the mantra. This signified that for anyone doing a corporate job just to make money, pay the bills or get through the day in the most unchallenging way possible – that there was more. A realisation that there had to be more to their dreams, hopes and education than that.

So, what was missing in the balance of having a well paid job, with a good company in a great office building? How about connection, development and personal growth and achievement? It is easy to use such words in the hope that by saying them the benefits are absorbed by osmosis, but in reality the process of growth and change is not always an easy one. Just as we relate to our families and friends, we each must learn to relate honestly with ourselves. Clear communication comes from that honesty as we express how we feel and what we need. If strategies for office interrelations were as developed as financial strategies, the work environment would be one of harmony, productivity and happiness. Nothing is more productive than people who work because they want to. If people are given autonomy and learn to self-appraise then they begin to take responsibility for themselves, their work and consequently their environment.

Within minutes of seeing the second building collapse I found myself outside near Ground Zero carrying 50lb bags of ice, trays of coffee and tea, jars of pain killers and bottles of water. The police and fire services were in need of constant support. They were holding one another and crying. I was with them for hours that day, but was filled with an overwhelming sense of helplessness. I didn't want to get on a plane and 'come home where it's safe', I wanted to stay amongst the people who had been bonded by this common experience. Barriers were broken down and everyone was unified, appreciative, warm, communicative and helpful. I felt like a New Yorker. I felt like a real part of the community. Everyone was working together because they wanted to, they desperately wanted to.

As the dust settles over Manhattan lives are changed forever but, despite the huge personal loss and tragedy, there are thousands of people who have re-evaluated their lives and priorities.

The heart and soul are being addressed in terms of new career possibilities because life is about relationship; relationship to ourselves, within ourselves, with objects and other people. The sooner we all learn to develop our relationship skills the healthier and happier our worlds will be. Work should not be a separate part of our lives but an integral part of our development and learning. As all the men and woman who ran from the falling buildings that day in September will testify, 'life is just too short'.

And as for me; a month later I returned to London 'where it was safe', back to my comfortable flat, new job, old friends – and then I began the process of giving it all up. Within months I had sold most of my possessions, left my job, said goodbye to my friends and was on a plane back to New York. And so here I am. No real job, staying with different people hoping to find a place to unpack my bags, slowly making friends and a new life. Of course it's not easy. All I know is that this is what my heart and soul needed to do. I don't know what lies ahead for me here but talking to strangers and being open to the potentiality in the moment is the best way for me to connect to my experience. I could have played it safe and stayed within my secure environment for the next 30 years but then I would be missing out on all the lessons, adventures, new people, new self and opportunities which come when we each step out into the unknown, even if it is only for a moment.

*Morgaine is currently completing her PhD and is trying to
make a new life for herself by following her dreams in NYC.
Her throat is sore from a great jazz singing class she has found.
morgaine_g@hotmail.com*

MORGAINE GAYE
A Reflection

There's something in the great stories that make you want to be there. When my little boy Sam tells me he is too scared to listen again to the tape of *Jack and the Beanstalk* (but really wants me to put it on again), it's because he can propel himself into the tale. He can see the Giant descending the stalk towards the end, threatening to stamp everything to kingdom come.

But he can't see him of course. It's all in his head.

Nor can I really know what it was like for Morgaine to step out of her apartment one typically hot September morning into the fantastic world she was about to inhabit.

All those of us who watched 9/11 from whatever remove, but were not actually there, do not know what it was really like – even though it left us deeply in shock. (And as a facilitator I've experienced, so often since, the ripples of human grief – in so many unexpected ways in seemingly unconnected scenarios – that the September events created around the world.)

We had a meeting with a PR company as we were writing *My Voodoo*. I ventured to describe the book as 'a self-help manual for a post-9/11 world', meaning that I hoped it would be full of the complexity and intensity that the event symbolised. I remember the response I had: "Oh Lordy, let's not go back to that; we've moved on, haven't we?"

I hope we haven't. Until we've understood what it was truly all about (and I haven't yet, have you?), we have no right to say to our ancestors that we are happy to move on…

And yet there's Morgaine, moving on, at whatever pace is best for her (and not the pace the rest of us demand when we want things to be 'normal' again)…

And her report from the edge?

An embracing of ambiguity and complexity:

'…the potentiality in the moment is the best way for me to connect to my experience. I could have played it safe and stayed within my secure environment for the next 30 years…'

But she hasn't. Have you?

What event does it take for you not to?

YOUR REFLECTION ON THIS STORY

ELVIN K BOX
"Give Peace, and conflict, a chance": My Own Personal Voodoo

My corporate bosses told me back in March 2001 that my probationary period was to be extended by another three months, because I was too lateral in my thinking. I was too creative, too loud, too boisterous, too different, too happy, too much of everything in fact, except... corporate. At the time I was engaged as a Project Manager, served my probationary period with the proverbial lid on it and then signed on the dotted line as one who had obviously seen the errors of his ways. Well, so they thought. I have a mortgage, kids and other assorted debts. I just went into hibernation!

Yeah, so, soon got moved into the Information Systems Manager job, because they needed someone who had 'imagination, ideas, prepared to confront the technological age and ride with his head out of the window whilst hurtling along the information highway!' Excellent, now we are getting somewhere.

Or rather not.

Come September 11th, whilst Manhattan was under attack by zealots worshipping an irrational Lord and Master, my corporate world was under a less destructive attack, but still by people who danced to the tune of lunatics. The organisation had to show the analysts in the City they worshipped at their altar, and promptly went into downsize mode. Get with the business model which is sexy.

Under threat of redundancy, because I didn't 'fit' the role in their brave new world, I hawked my talents around the organisation to see if they could find a home. At the eleventh hour, with my redundancy cheque winging its way into my bank account, a lifeline was thrown. They needed a Marketing Manager, because the 'suited and booted' ones they had decided to leave when the going got tough.

The moral of the story is thus – like it or not these are 100% crazy times, and again, like it or not, you just gotta employ a 'crazee' to combat such an environment. The ones who feel the fear and do it anyway. Those that are not fazed by change in any way, shape or form. Get in the people who communicate in every sense of the word – face-to-face, via email, over the phone, through ad-hoc posters on the office wall. In a nutshell those who revel in their lust for life and inspire those around them with humour, spirituality, passion and a child-like curiosity that constantly begs the question 'why?'

They may be crazy, but by God they are adaptable. They may seem completely nuts to those who conform and are termed 'conventional', but they have the ability to learn, are not held back by the past and have the imagination to apply their off-the-wall wisdom to enable the future.

So the next time you decide to have a cull of your staff, start with those who are 'regular', wear suits and obey without question. Leave the 'crazees' right where they are, because as of now there is no such thing as 'fit'. The roles of the future have not been thought of yet, and nor has the corporate business model. More to the point, there are not enough of these wild, effervescent 'crazees' to go around!

The business world lives on the edge of chaos, where creativity is a natural by-product. Best you employ, support, encourage a bunch of Mavericks to aid and inspire such creativity amongst those less fortunate souls who can only adapt, not innovate. These 'characters', with their jocular nature and seemingly abrasive and undisciplined approach to corporate life, may be seen as 'Fools', but they are not 'Buffoons'. Let me tell ya, they live a million miles from a town called Stupid and empathise with the real world. One which they, the poor and meek shall probably inherit.

Elvin Box currently works for a UK based construction consultancy, whose clients include Railtrack, Lend Lease, Carillion and BP.
elvin@schal.co.uk

ELVIN K BOX
A Reflection

Breathless, excited, says-it-like-he-sees-it, totally idiosyncratic. Elvin's been corresponding with me since my Corporate Fool days, when I did a presentation at BP.

What I like about listening to Elvin is that he shows us two sides of the maverick/magician promise. On one side he reminds us that you've got to have huge self-confidence and pretty unflappable self-esteem to be a maverick. Someone who does not have those things would not like being on the 'outside' of things so much. Elvin is high on the upbeat scale. And that alone would make him stand out in many of our organisational cultures. Negativity we can handle, uniform emotion at all times we will ask for, cynicism we can tolerate as if it were oxygen; but get someone in the group who is positive and upbeat and we shift in our chairs, embarrassed.

The other side is that all that upbeatness does make people uncomfortable. And that has issues, not just for the maverick him or herself, but also for the people working with or managing them.

Would you want the Elvins of this world in your team? If not, why not? When does your corporate recruitment policy eliminate the deviants? When does your personal comfort zone dampen diversity? And, when it does, where does the innovation and challenge come from?

YOUR REFLECTION ON THIS STORY

ANDREW ROSS
Valued Experience?

In the mid 1990s I joined the General Electric Company as a member of the management team for a new business unit in the UK. At the time, GE was amongst the 4 largest companies in the world posting around $80b annual revenue and $7b profit. It was also one of the most diverse commercial organisations on the planet.

My immediate boss was an American, in his 50s and a long serving GE employee. At interview and on my first day in the company, he talked passionately about GE values: the three Ss (Speed, Simplicity and Self-confidence); boundaryless behaviour; anti-bureaucracy; empowerment; reality; integrity, informality; differentiation; diversity; workout; stretch and the GE currency (its shares). We didn't discuss hard targets or budgets for the business, just how it would feel, what sort of people it needed and the values to which it would work.

Later that first day I watched a video of GE's then CEO, Jack Welch, speaking to the company's Senior Executives at their annual conference in Boca Raton. I later learned that this 'State of The Union' address was filmed every year for all of GE's 240,000 employees to watch during the following months.

For over an hour, I listened to one of the world's leading Chief Executives talking earnestly about the values my immediate boss had described. Jack Welch spoke about them and about people in a way which elevated their importance far above financial targets and operating plans. Strategic stuff was covered, but always related back to the company's core values.

What really struck me was the fact this wasn't a video put together as part of an induction programme. I'd heard 'people are our greatest asset' and 'my door is always open' clichés on my first days in other organisations. But this was a film of the CEO ramming home messages to his top team at their biggest operational meeting of the year.

Secondly, none of Jack Welch's passion had been diluted as it flowed down the management structure to my boss. The values were as meaningful to managers in the field as they were to the person at the top. They would define the way I ran my operations – as they did in the hundreds of other GE business units in over 100 countries around the globe.

Previously I had worked in companies, both large and small, which didn't attend to the sort of values I was now hearing about or paid them lip service because they were a distraction from real commercial issues. As a result, and by default, a staid, narrow and restrictive culture developed in those organisations. But these were the businesses with which I had become familiar and it came as a complete surprise to find one of the world's most successful companies so focused on 'soft' issues. It didn't take me long to realise that GE was successful because it was focused on core values. Rather than being 'soft' issues, they were granite bedrock for the whole organisation.

Over the next few years I observed GE values in action. I witnessed:

◆ The company ditch business leaders, who were making their numbers, because they didn't demonstrate commitment to company values.
◆ Individuals promoted and rewarded handsomely because they delivered results in the right way – motivating others, sharing success and doing it all with passion.
◆ Ideas flow across business units, across market sectors and across continents as though they were being shared between people sitting next to one another.
◆ The company change fundamental operating practices and targets because someone from outside the organisation suggested a better way.
◆ Revolutionary new initiatives such as Six Sigma and e-business driven so quickly that many single-site organisations would have found it difficult to match the pace.
◆ The very best people applied to any and every new initiative.
◆ Courses and meetings attended by individuals of both sexes and of differing seniority, nationality and experience who were always genuinely able to participate on equal terms.
◆ Ideas generated on the shop floor and embraced all the way to the highest levels of the organisation.
◆ GE stock become an ever more valuable commodity to investors and the only true currency within the business.
◆ Leaders willing to be challenged.
◆ Business units take risks and occasionally fail, yet never lose their direction or support from above.
◆ Employees receive a pat on the back for having the determination, guts and passion to try something with potential – even when it didn't work out.

- Business leaders always wanting to see and hear the truth – good or bad.
- Leaders getting out into the business units, meeting with employees and continually promoting the GE way.

These weren't just things I observed occasionally. They were a part of everyday life. It was the way GE operated – and still does. Throughout, Jack Welch reiterated the company values over and over again, speech after speech, year after year. Every GE employee knew exactly what the CEO believed in and what the company stood for. In some organisations for which I worked I was given a laminated card containing the company mission statement. At GE, I carried a card listing company values.

GE sometimes found itself with employees who just didn't 'get it' – some recruited, others who joined through acquisition. But employees who never took the GE way to their hearts would leave or be persuaded to do so. At any given point, there were pockets within the business where the sun didn't shine, but these soon became evident and were brought into the light.

If this sounds like a description of corporate utopia, it isn't. GE was not (and is still not) perfect. But nobody within GE ever thought it was. In fact, it's part of the core philosophy that there's always a better way. Whatever a business or individual is doing, somebody, somewhere, will find the means to do it cheaper, faster or more accurately, and the source might not be an obvious one. Even for those currently enjoying best practice, today's solutions won't be good enough tomorrow – understanding that is crucial, and a fundamental GE principle.

Perhaps the rule is better proven by companies which don't employ those values. They significantly outnumber the businesses which do, and I've had experience of a representative sample.

There are many examples of organisations with the wrong values. I have a story about one where an absence of values has had a devastating impact. It's a personal story about the Energis Group, a telecommunications company I have worked for and which I know well.

The Energis Group grew significantly through acquisition. Planet Online, a major UK Internet hosting business, was acquired in 1998 and re-branded as Energis Squared. Both Energis Squared and the wider Group enjoyed much success and rapid growth over a relatively short period both prior to, and immediately after acquisition. In 2000, The Energis Group was a FTSE 100 listed company valued at around £12b.

But there were two underlying cultural problems. The first was born out of speed of growth. Energis Squared had grown very rapidly from green-field start-up. In the early days it enjoyed all the benefits of a small, fast moving organisation – informality, idea-flow, empowerment and anti-bureaucratic behaviour. Not because these were consciously built into the company's culture: they simply emerged by default because a small group of motivated people was making things happen. In such situations, people don't need to rationalise the values at work; they just naturally function a certain way.

But as the company grew things changed. The workforce increased to over 600; single-site operations became multi-site; functions separated; additional management layers were created, financial constraints were introduced and the leader became ever more distant from the business and its people. Longer serving employees felt the changes and the effects they were having but no remedies were applied. The leader really needed to consciously establish values, which would keep all the small company advantages alive – values such as speed, simplicity, informality, anti-bureaucracy, reality, and something akin to the GE workout initiative. But none of this ever happened.

It's not entirely surprising that a leader should miss this requirement if he or she has previously only had to think about what the organisation does rather than how it does it. But understanding the failure doesn't make it any less devastating. Within Energis, the problem only worsened as the leader became more isolated and less accessible to suggestions from those who could see what was missing.

The second problem resulted from acquisition by the Energis Group and affected both parent and adopted child. Neither operated on strong, progressive values, instead having weak cultures, which had evolved by default. But the two cultures were different and, in the absence of a common set of values to guide the organisation, they never mixed. This created numerous problems, even in customer-facing activities.

Valueless companies can change – it's never too late. Sometimes there has to be a change of leadership but that's not inevitable. Chief Executives whose leadership is wanting can suddenly become converts to a set of values, which makes all the difference. But such conversions need to take place in the heart and not just in the head.

Energis Squared had one such moment for change in June 2001. The Business Leader and Marketing Director realised the company was losing its ability to innovate. This was borne out by figures which proved that the proportion of revenue being generated from new products and services was declining rapidly. The company needed to rediscover the innovative approach, which defined its early years when it revolutionised the UK Internet market with products such as Freeserve, launched in conjunction with Dixons.

Admirably, these two key Energis Squared executives arranged a two-day workshop at the Earth Centre in Doncaster – a unique, inspirational venue. The event was attended by the top 50 or so managers from within the company and facilitated by outside consultants. The intention was to debate ideas – off-the-wall ideas – about what would make the company more innovative and to end the two days with half a dozen immediate projects which would make the greatest difference, and to develop a pipeline of future actions.

The concept was brilliant. This could and should have been a defining moment for the organisation – the dawning of a new era. Some managers attending were sceptical that the company was committed to change but others, like myself, were optimistic that results would prove otherwise.

The event got off to the worst possible start. The Chief Executive opened proceedings with a ten-minute speech about its importance – and then left! In my lifetime within the company, it was the one and only time he created the opportunity to engage with a group of managers other than his direct reports, and he gave it only ten minutes and a one-way conversation.

The second problem arose when we started what were supposedly no-holds-barred breakout sessions. I spoke passionately about the need for corporate values, driven from the top which would allow the organisation to think, feel and act like a small company again. I talked about my experiences in GE and examples of how corporate values drove successful strategic planning and tactical operations. For me, this was the most crucial issue for us to consider and grounds for a series of actions, which would revolutionise the business. By the end of the two days, I would have settled for just one pipeline project.

The Marketing Director stated that company values were a matter for the Group CEO and the Energis Squared Business Leader, one of whom would issue a statement at some point in the future, and at that point, the debate moved on. Eight months later, no leadership statement on corporate values has been made.

We ended the two-day workshop with six specific projects, all of them perfectly valid and some which could have been steered to deliver cultural change. Sadly, all died a lingering death without delivering anything. Why that happened becomes clear from the second phase of the story.

The Energis Squared Business Leader and Marketing Director both discovered *Corporate Voodoo*. They liked what they read and could rationalise many of the messages it contained. In hindsight it's obvious that neither of them really 'got it', but I was once more filled with optimism, hoping the Voodoo principles I had also read about would take root within Energis.

A grand event was arranged to launch the Innovation initiative to the rest of the company and René Carayol was invited as the keynote speaker. René gave what most people concurred was a truly motivational talk on Voodoo principles and cited examples of those values in action and of failing companies where they were missing. It's regrettable and indicative that less than one third of the company's employees turned up for the event.

For me, the most telling moment came when René said to the assembled audience that whilst he heard Energis Squared leaders talking Voodoo, he didn't detect any passion. Neither the Business Leader nor any member of his senior team got up to challenge René's comment. Nor did they answer him when he questioned the company's diversity and the make-up of its management team. At that point, I realised they were just humming along to the tune.

Since then the whole telecommunications sector has taken a beating but the Energis Group has suffered more than most. Commercially, it was in a more sound position than many of its competitors at the outset of the market decline, but it hadn't the leadership or the corporate values through which to find answers to the growing challenges. Instead there was protectionism, defensiveness and arrogance in abundance.

It's very easy to blame the Energis collapse on market factors, some bad financial decisions, especially over-commitment in continental Europe, and inappropriate focusing of the sales team. But whilst they are certainly key factors, they are only symptoms of a wider failing. The leadership was out of touch; there was no ability to draw-out innovative solutions; leaders were not willing to accept challenge and there wasn't enough diverse thinking. With different corporate values, the organisation would have dealt more effectively with the commercial challenges it, and the whole market sector, was facing. As it is, Energis now holds the distinction of a record loss on the FTSE index, having seen £500m wiped off its market value in one three hour spell. A business valued at £12b only two years ago is valued at £40m at this moment with a share price of 3p. The Energis Squared Business Leader and Marketing Director have both left the company and the organisation is fighting for its survival.

I am convinced that a company which ignores its culture and corporate values will fail or, at best, stumble along in mediocrity. Other factors influence the situation, but don't determine the fundamental position. On the flip side, companies which focus on the right corporate values always find a competitive solution and achieve success.

For me personally, the challenge is promoting that message to business leaders and senior executives who don't instinctively feel the same. It's something I have tried to do over the last few years, both from inside organisations and as an external consultant. It's not a question of making a rational case – most people can see sense in values which successful companies prove to be effective. Instead, there are two main difficulties.

The first is the fact that many Chief Executives genuinely believe they already operate to those values. However, whilst they may accept them at a conceptual level they don't 'feel' them, which is a bad combination. It means the values are never driven into the organisation but the leader doesn't see they are missing. And because he or she isn't instinctively committed to informality, reality, diversity and self-confidence, it makes it very difficult for subordinates or outside consultants to make the case.

The second difficulty arises where leaders see corporate values as 'soft, fluffy stuff' and a distraction from real commercial issues. I can understand that perspective, but it's a reversal of the truth. As successful businesses prove, getting culture, values and people right assures effective, competitive solutions on an ongoing basis.

There is one final issue, which troubles me personally – the risk of appearing arrogant. I feel passionate about the things I have outlined and I believe it's important that people should demonstrate passion. But there's a thin line to tread when offering passionate advice about leadership skills and corporate values, the wrong side of which is arrogance. The ability to always see that line and remain on the right side is one of my greatest challenges.

Arrogance in business is a terminal condition. Whilst the values in which I believe are designed to counter it, in promoting those values I may appear arrogant – something I think of as 'the arrogance paradox'. I recognise that leading a business requires many talents, amongst them financial acumen, negotiating skills and a gut instinct for dealmaking. Cultural values make up only one skill – it just happens to be my area of expertise and also the foundation stone of corporate success.

Reading *Corporate Voodoo* was a defining moment for me, as was hearing René present Voodoo concepts in person. It helped me crystallize many of my own views and introduced me to some new ideas. René is an experienced CEO and a strong personality who immediately commands respect amongst other business leaders whether they 'get' the messages he promotes or not. But for me, one of the most important voodoo principles is that 'practitioners punch way above their weight'. People who live Voodoo concepts and are passionate about them can make a difference on a large scale. I see the truth in that, but still wonder how Voodoo practitioners from a lowly background can best make their voices heard and avoid 'the arrogance paradox'?

Andrew still works with Energis.
andrew.ross@energis.com

ANDREW ROSS
A Reflection

Livid again. I had just had another glimpse of what life could be like for the disabled in the UK. My speaking agent had just called with an event in Leeds for Energis Squared. They were very interested in hearing the Voodoo principles. They had read the book and believed that they were very much in line with where they wanted to take their business. I happened to be very interested in the telecoms industry and very curious about the new kids on the block like Energis. Great, this was going to be very interesting and felt like fun.

The booking for the event was made through an events management company who wanted to meet with me for a final 'inspection' and to brief me. I had recently snapped my Achilles tendon playing squash, and so was on crutches. The whole meeting and subsequent conversations were about my ability to walk up steps and cope with a circular stage that demanded me moving around to face a 360-degree audience. We never really discussed what I was going to say and how I was going to do it. Eventually, I just had to say that I would be off crutches by then. I had become seriously over-sensitive because people never held doors open for me when I was on crutches. Nobody helped you with bags at airports. It was lonely and stressful. However, at least I could do my work. Or could I?

When the day arrived to go to Energis Squared, I was still on crutches and in plaster. But I had huge shoulders and biceps by now and could hurl myself enormous distances at frightening speed. I was a seriously menacing sight; people were frozen into keeping those doors open as I propelled myself towards them.

Energis Squared were desperate to brief me in detail about the message they wanted delivering. I spoke to the Business Leader and the Marketing Director at length a couple of times. They were smashing guys, who really cared about what they were trying to achieve. The Marketing Director was very conscious of how people felt. He was absolutely committed to changing this and making a positive difference. The Business Leader was also aware of this, but was a little more concerned with having a well-managed and well-run event. He was really the owner of the event but had been sucked into the process cornflakes and was not really thinking about the potential of the event for all of the people.

In a subsequent telephone call the Marketing Director and I discussed and agreed that it would be necessary and appropriate for me to provide some feedback based on my feelings and views on them.

The event was in a great environment. People turned up – the team did not. There was no team. The management and the people spoke completely different languages, especially body language. Arms were folded; faces were cold, no applause, and constant muttering all the way through the management speeches. All the managers spoke from autocue and there was negligible eye contact with the audience. They spoke at them, but it was done ever so well. The absolute nadir and major moment of truth was when the relatively new Group Chief Executive could not be there and delivered a 'heartfelt' message by video. I am sure he meant what he said, and I am also sure that he did not intend to patronise and talk down to his people. He outlined his view of a great future, and how integral his people were to achieving the Promised Land. The murmurings of discontent were at their loudest during the video.

I eventually limped on with crutches and spoke for an hour. This was a passion-free zone. I shared this with them. It was fairly obvious that there were endemic issues. Anger was in the air. There were no common goals. There was no vision. There was definitely no inspiration.

There were four monitors acting as autocues, in clear view of everybody in the arena. The audience were patronised by the fact that even motherhood and apple pie needed scripting. They mockingly mouthed the words as the executives said their pieces.

The final insult and condemnation of the management was when all read the closing words, which were meant to motivate, before they were said.

Energis are seemingly in their death throes at the moment. Their banks now hold the future of Energis and its people in their lending talks and discussions. This is unfortunate and may have been unavoidable; however, the management did not need to lead the cavalry charge to destruction in such a reckless manner. Andrew has given an eloquent insight into the value of values.

In *Corporate Voodoo* we examined corporate culture and the necessity of having an open culture. We have now looked at the impact of differing cultures on individuals.

Andrew has shared with us his own powerful Voodoo.

What is your story? And how will it end?

HELEN MULLEN
The Reality of Voodoo

So what does Voodoo mean to a fast growing, opinionated company, full of energy and a diverse range of people and skills?

New Media Partners do Voodoo! But why?

I read the book at the right time, in the right place and for the wrong reasons. It looked interesting on the bookshelves and conjured up images of the James Bond film, *Live and Let Die* (as I said, not necessarily the right reasons)!

Anyway, it proved to be a page-turner and, having read it within the space of a plane journey, I found Voodoo-speak had entered my vocabulary.

The book made its way around the office and generated lots of feedback. Other copies of *Corporate Voodoo* were sent to clients and associates who were curious to find out what it was all about – another mad Mullen idea?

Some got it. Some didn't. Some were hooked. Others dropped off. But all had something to say including invitations to 'drink blood and dance the night away!'

In our organisation, we set up a weekly Voodoo meeting that embodied how we collectively viewed Voodoo. A forum for us to come together and unleash the magic! Different backgrounds, different skill sets, different roles and different personalities in one room to discuss topics that inspired us (or not!) – all facilitated by several refreshments! This gave us a way of not only exploring interesting subjects together but also enabled us to bond together as a group and gain more insight into each other's world.

Overall, it gave everyone an opportunity to generate ideas without fear of being perceived as mad, wacky, off the wall, rocking the boat and all the other adjectives that are often rolled out when magic starts to work and people get uncomfortable.

We continue to Voodoo at nmp. It has even been highlighted as a positive thing during our recent Investors In People award. It has changed from the pure magic that I found on the plane journey; however that's what Voodoo should do – reinvent, challenge, inspire and move to better things. A bit like our nmp mantra: think…inspire…do…

Helen Mullen
New Media Partners Ltd
helen@newmediapartners.co.uk

HELEN MULLEN
A Reflection

Helen delivers a beautiful and simple approach to utilising Voodoo in her organisation. It has fitted nicely into the culture of a 'fast growing, opinionated company, full of energy and a diverse range of people and skills'. Having now met some of the practitioners at nmp, it is easy to see why Voodoo works for them. They work in a world of little precedence, and certainly few sacred cows. They are a dynamic team who really do like working with each other. They are brave enough to be selective about the work they take on, and what they do not.

There is nothing too complex about their approach to Voodoo, but as with most things, they enjoy doing it, so therefore they do it well, and they do it well, so they enjoy doing it. The Virtuous Voodoo Circle!

YOUR REFLECTION ON THIS STORY

So here's decision time. On pages 98-9 you made three conclusions and three commitments for each Voodoo question.

In *Corporate Voodoo* we described a nine-step plan for 'making it happen'. Now how will *you* make the magic happen?

VOODOO CHECKLIST REVISITED 1: THE NINE STEPS TO MAKING THINGS HAPPEN

1. You've reviewed your influencing skills – you've mastered the tools of persuasion and communication, the only thing you have for making your dreams a reality.

2. You've tackled your fear of failure e.g. 'I tried it before and it didn't work' 'if I fail, people will think I'm stupid' 'if I fail, I'll think I'm stupid'

Implications for Voodoo Question One

Implications for Voodoo Question One

Implications for Voodoo Question Two

Implications for Voodoo Question Two

Implications for Voodoo Question Three

Implications for Voodoo Question Three

3. **You've tackled your fear of success e.g. 'I don't deserve to succeed because I've conditioned myself into unworthiness'**

'I don't want to succeed, because actually I like things the way they are'

'I don't want to succeed, because if I do it will bring me new challenges and responsibilities'

'If I'm successful, it will mean more effort and energy to sustain success'

'If I'm successful, people won't give me their sympathy and keep saying "oh, I know", "oh, you're right" and "there, there, never mind".'

Implications for Voodoo Question One

Implications for Voodoo Question Two

Implications for Voodoo Question Three

4. **You've a vision of exactly what you want to achieve, have translated that into a benefits package for your customers/audience and then into a 'small steps/how to get there' plan**

Implications for Voodoo Question One

Implications for Voodoo Question Two

Implications for Voodoo Question Three

5. **You work only on what lies within your circle of influence. You learn from and disregard the rest. And you're prepared to be flexible in your approach, so you arm yourself with counter-arguments, Plan Bs etc**

Implications for Voodoo Question One

Implications for Voodoo Question Two

Implications for Voodoo Question Three

6. **You've taken feedback from colleagues and garnered advice from 'experts'**

Implications for Voodoo Question One

Implications for Voodoo Question Two

Implications for Voodoo Question Three

7. **You've chosen your time and place for taking action wisely**

Implications for Voodoo Question One

Implications for Voodoo Question Two

Implications for Voodoo Question Three

8. If the response is not what you want, you know you will either persevere – with enquiry, creativity and tact – or you will learn from it and let go

Implications for Voodoo Question One

Implications for Voodoo Question Two

Implications for Voodoo Question Three

9. You know that nothing will happen on your idea unless YOU make a stand for it

Implications for Voodoo Question One

Implications for Voodoo Question Two

Implications for Voodoo Question Three

...so what are you waiting for?

Voodoo
Steps
outside....

Having made our decisions on the Voodoo Questions, having connected with others who can teach us more about ourselves, we are ready to step outside and meet our destiny.

Outside we will, inevitably, meet the world of organisations and business and all that this entails. Out of *Corporate Voodoo*, into *My Voodoo* and back again. Full circle.

In this fifth section of *My Voodoo*, we offer our views on six aspects of organisational life from a Voodoo perspective. Each of these essays was written in direct response to questions we received during Q&A sessions at Voodoo consulting or speaking events. They were the things that were important to people at that moment in time. "Yes, yes," they'd say, "but what about dealing with office politics...?" or "How would you give an appraisal, then?"

Next we give a list of questions we'd ask of any company starting up and wanting to make its mark in the world.

And there follows a similar list of questions that might just Voodoo-ise your team, if you're not careful.

Next, we return to a final checklist from *Corporate Voodoo*, and invite you to apply it your team, organisation or group. By embracing these ten principles, how could your offering, your promise to the world, be enhanced and deepened?

If you decide to have any influence in your organisation, however big or small it may be, we ask you to consider our take on the world of business. Business does not always have to be as it has always been.

Finally, we step back into the pages of *Corporate Voodoo* from a new perspective, looking again at the Fast and Slow companies we described there, and ending with a very personal account of one of Voodoo's key themes: honour the children (because that's where the future lies)…

Towards the Voodoo Organisation 1

ACQUIRING THE SCARY TALENT

Take away my people, but leave my factories,
and soon grass will grow on the factory floors.
Take away my factories, but leave my people,
and soon we will have a new and better factory.
Andrew Carnegie

It used to be that the scarcest commodity in business was stuff like oil or coal. Competitive advantage came from being the company who could get nearest to the black stuff first. Then the scarcest commodity for a time was customers – could your company get a powerful market share? At the start of the e-commerce age, the scarcest commodity was finance – could you persuade the venture capitalists that their money was more wisely invested in your start-up than in the one down the road?

Now the scarcest commodity is people. Not just any people, but the right people – the right stuff.

The 'next economy' companies can't recruit talented people fast enough and the consequent talent shortage is the biggest obstacle they face to the ambitious growth targets they've set themselves becoming a reality (Netscape went from 2 to 2000 employees in its first three years).

But this not just a numbers game; it is more about getting the right people, not just herds of lemmings. Think personality first, and think skills second – we can always train and develop to meet any skills shortfall. There is little that can be done with the wrong personalities apart from fire them.

And finding a way to overcome this obstacle is companies' greatest priority.

Your company may or may not feel that it is a 'new economy' organisation, desperate for the hottest new e-talent, but whether you're producing widgets, software or cheese, as a leader you are responsible for bringing the most competent people available into your organisation. Your product or service – and your day-to-day sanity – is only as healthy as the people on your team.

And it won't just be a question of whether the new people you find have the right skills or technical know-how; you'll need to be sure that they have the right attitudes and characteristics to fit into your current team and the wider organisational culture.

So what's the secret to hiring the best people into your organisation?

The major ingredient is mindset. Doing what we always have done is not necessarily a recipe for success no matter what our role or business. It is not just about being different for difference's sake. It is about how to do things in a manner that both exploits and capitalises upon existing strengths and capabilities, but adding to this what customers are demanding, what new competitors are pledging to do, what technology has now made possible. Remember, it is rare now that measurements of business success are internal. They tend to be set by the stakeholder community, YOUR stakeholder community; shareholders, customers, employees, suppliers, local community etc.

Consequently, we should all feel encouraged to look for talent in places we have never looked before. People we would previously have dismissed at a glance may now have a part to play in our future growth and success. Think New Ideas and Scary People! Who would have believed ten years ago that an open marketeer, not born of the socialist tendency, without a love affair with the trade union movement, would be the most successful Labour Party leader ever? Not forgetting his having a fashionable and successful wife!

Think the unthinkable, do the undoable. Think Sven-Goran Eriksson?

Here follows the Voodoo User's Guide to Acquiring Scary Talent...

THE TEN COMMITMENTS OF TALENT ACQUISITION

I. Thou Shalt sort out the difference between skills and personality, and experience and courage

Loosen your organisation's obsession with skills and past performance. A candidate's experience and skills are relevant, but what is most relevant is the person sitting in front of you. They may have a lot more to offer in the right environment with the right support.

II. Thou Shalt communicate your brand proposition

It is essential that in a competitive world for the best talent, those potential candidates understand your strengths and your commitment to careers. The compelling reason why a talented person would want to work for your company is usually represented by your brand values. Orange does this without moving its lips!

III. Thou Shalt identify the living embodiment of the brand

It is important to understand which person in the organisation is the best symbol for your brand. When Virgin are chasing a real big hitter it is no surprise that they wheel out Sir Richard as their ace in the pack. Why? Because he and Virgin stand for: young at heart, consumer champion, anti-establishment, sexy, entrepreneurial, winners. This may not be exactly true, but brands are about building perceptions. Who is your Sir Richard?

IV. Thou Shalt be governed by the external, not the internal, environment

Packages, salaries, bonus elements must be calibrated against your competitors and the market leaders in your sector. Worry less about who earns what internally.

V. Thou Shalt Not let the socially inept recruit for you

The recruiters are sometimes the only representatives of your organisation that potential candidates will have met. What impression are they creating and, more importantly, leaving the candidates with?

VI. Thou Shalt act incisively and decisively on offers

In a fast moving world, we are looking for incisive and decisive people. Taking three months over the decision making process for employment is probably a telling symptom of your prevailing culture. A rapid decision, positive or negative, will add currency to how your organisation is perceived in the jobs marketplace. Candidates prefer to fail fast! Make people feel important, make recruitment companies feel important: unsurprisingly, they will give you their best in return.

VII. Thou Shalt employ diverse search tactics

The talent you need may be alive and well and living in your organisation. It may not be called 'manager'. Talent may not have gone to the right university and it may not have gone into further education at all. Talent may think and act in the right manner, but may dress in an unusual way. Talent may not speak in the same way as the people in the organisation do. These are not barriers to success.

VIII. Thou Shalt ask your existing employees

Your people will add value to establishing the attributes that they feel are important for success. They may also know the people who could make the telling difference!

IX. Thou Shalt Not clone exclusively

It is imperative to have your own talent pool to dip into for your succession plans. Too much of this can lead to inbreeding. No organisation has a monopoly on talent in the New Millennium.

X. Thou Shalt Not, having got your talent, feel the need to keep it forever

There are too many current examples of where the desire for low staff turnover rates and loyalty as a measurement of organisational success has led to stagnation, especially at senior levels. We have recently seen shareholders and non-executive directors having to intervene and encourage senior executives to 'spend more time with their families'. It is not damaging to move on after a period of sustained success, or otherwise.

Change is optional because survival is not mandatory.
Lord Denning

THREE GOOD THINGS TO LOOK FOR IN A CV:

1. How did the CV make you feel after you had read it?
> Did you feel excited?
> Was there a sense of urgency translated?
> Did a clear confidence in their own abilities come through?
> Was there any indication of passion for the businesses they worked in?

2. The accompanying letter is as important as the CV.
> Was there any evidence of having researched your business or organisation?
> Was this a general mail shot or one that was specifically targeted?
> Did you feel that the approach adopted said anything unique about the writer?
> Remember we are trying to think personality, not just skills.

3. Think contribution NOT past experience.
> The more senior the role, the more your real requirement is not only what difference they have made in the past but, far more importantly, what difference they could make to keeping your business going forward. Think future contribution NOT just past performance.

FIVE GOOD QUESTIONS TO ASK IN AN INTERVIEW:

1.Where would you like to be in three years time?

What will you have achieved in life (including business)?

How will this position/organisation assist you in achieving those goals?

Remember without common goals you really do not have a team!

2. Given a blank sheet of paper, what are the activities that would make a great day for you (include domestics and personal stuff)?

This should reveal a lot about what their natural strengths are; we all like to do what we are good at.

3. Who are your life role models (include business and private)?

This can be indicative about the management style of the individual. Any mention of Tim McVeigh should raise some concerns!

4. Tell me about the last three mistakes you have made and how you dealt with them?

Remember making mistakes is healthy, as long as there is no human carnage involved.

5. Are you a Roundhead or Cavalier?

Do you need the comfort of process, or are you more at home breaking the rules?

There is no right or wrong; just be clear on what you need, not what you want.

Towards the Voodoo Organization 2

SUCCESSION PLANNING
The future belongs to those who plan for it today
Anon

Succession planning always seems to be something we'll think about next year, until a key management player disappears and his or her replacement must be found in an unseemly hurry. When Matalan's widely respected CEO, Angus Monroe, suddenly departed the impact on the company's performance and share value was plain to see. When BT lost its CEO and its CFO, it had no obvious successors in the frame. Succession planning can avoid chaotic baton changes. But more positively, good planning can add value, not just avoid loss.

Tesco in-house legend has it that when Ian McLaurin was CEO he spotted Terry Leahy, the present chief, working as a marketing executive. McLaurin started grooming Leahy for the top job years in advance of the need. Even though John Brown still has seven years left at the helm of BP, it's widely believed that the search for his successor has already begun. This may be excessively prudent, but at least BP should avoid the unseemly public fracas that arose when Rick Greenbury departed from M&S.

The best leaders in business are not only good talent spotters, but also talent magnets. Start now putting that ability to work. Remember that the next generation of leaders will face different challenges. Don't just settle for replacing today's leaders with their younger clones. Remember when Kevin Keegan turned his back on the England manager's job? Because there was no succession plan, the FA had to cope with the problems of appointing a foreign manager while the search was going on. They got the right man by luck, not judgement. The French managerial team always contains two or three individuals who will be contenders for the top job, with the results we see: European and ex-World champions.

Look wide for talent. Look in unlikely places. Why is Bill Gates so successful? He's not a technical genius, nor (sorry, Bill) a particularly attractive personality. But he had a vision, which meant that thousands of talented people were eager to join Microsoft, and he's one of the greatest dealmakers in the world.

THE VOODOO GUIDE TO SUCCESSION PLANNING

◆ Make talent spotting an explicit task for managers at every level. Make your people think about it, work at it and report results.

◆ Look for talent in the likely and unlikely places.

◆ Demand the best. Don't forget Eisenhower's maxim on the eve of D-Day: If you're not sure you have the right officer in place, then you don't.

◆ Look for personal qualities, such as leadership, vision, communication skills, dealmaking. Don't be hypnotised by track record. One CEO said to me, "Our recruitment policy is simple. We hire on skills and fire on personality." Skills can be acquired. Personal qualities can't.

◆ Get some scary people in key roles. In the future, new ideas are the oxygen of the corporation. Bring in some cavaliers to challenge the management roundheads.

◆ Diversity works, especially in management. You don't need a team of centre-backs.

◆ Establish a high-flyer's club. People need to know if great things are expected of them, and to know early.

◆ Mentor and guide your crème de la crème. Send them on secondment to suppliers, customers and partners. Encourage them to get a wide vision.

◆ Drop the weakest link from the highflying cadre, if the evidence is strong. It's not a kindness to do otherwise.

◆ Try to get your most talented individuals working together on projects. You may be building tomorrow's board.

◆ Recognise and reward the best team builders.

◆ Never, ever, accept as an excuse for failure that 'I had a shortage of talent in my team'. Answer: 'It was your job to find the talent'. Great leaders like Columbus and Christ didn't look for people who'd been to America before, or founded a world religion before. They took talented people, provided inspiring leadership, and met their goals.

Towards the Voodoo Organization 3

GIVING GREAT APPRAISALS

This essay is in three sections: 'Understand the 'Why?', 'Think Strategic' and 'Be Tactical'. The first part is critical. There won't be a huge amount in the two checklists that follow that will surprise you (it is, we hope, to borrow Charles Handy's phrase, 'a blinding glimpse of the obvious'). But what we find works is that managers who are appraising need not so much be reminded what to do, but rather need to be enlightened on (or reconnected to) the purpose and role of appraisals. So here goes:

Understand the 'Why?'

In the space of a one-hour meeting, my boss took a highly motivated employee and made [me] highly unmotivated. **Anon**

The shadow of the school report card hangs over too many appraisals. Someone who is apparently superior to another is going to judge that other and tell them whether they're up to the mark. Performance appraisals are a classic business tradition where Muggle managers can reveal themselves – judgemental, backwards looking, and autocratic. Appraisals are not about ego, they are about coaching development.

People need an outlet for discussing themselves and how they are succeeding rather than just talking about their jobs and activities. Personal development leads to organisational growth. Any appraisal should primarily be a self-appraisal.

People need to know if they are on target against the goals they set themselves. Objective feedback is a good way of getting that, since self-perception is a potentially erratic critic.

An appraisal is not just a reflective ritual (assessing the past and putting meaning on it); it is a creative form. An appraisal creates goals, ambitions, plans and commitments that were not there before. Like your company, your appraisals should balance the past and the future.

Appraisals are for you as well as for the employee. Appraising people regularly is a way for you to generate an understanding of what's happening to the story people are telling about the business, their place in it and its future.

Then **Think Strategic**:

In today's environment, you have to evaluate what's changing and what's staying the same, what's working and what's no longer working. Feedback plays that role.
Bruce Tulgan

◆ Appraisals are about getting more for the organisation, the individual and the line manager giving the appraisal

◆ Appraisals are the probably the most important time to be honest and direct; weasel words here can be seriously detrimental for all concerned

◆ This is a time to both build and develop the individual and the team

◆ This is not a task; the appraisal says as much about the appraiser as about the individual – poorly managed and delivered appraisals are eloquent statements about the appraiser

◆ This is a time for honest succession management

◆ This is a time to decide not to hide

◆ Appraisals assist in building a vision/career for the individual

◆ Expect to be delighted, and propose success; don't define failure

◆ Encourage (en-courage: to make bold)

◆ This is not a Task, this is Development: do it in that spirit

◆ The environment and conversation needs to be fun and light, not heavy and confrontational (consider not doing appraisals in your office)

◆ Preparation is key; carefully given feedback should be enlightening and helpful, not penalising

◆ There must be no major surprises

◆ The appraisal is a forum for big decisions. How is this individual's future going to affect the context (the future of the team, the company, the strategy)?

And now, **Be Tactical**:

If you have ideas and information that will help someone perform better, it's hostile not to share them.
Anne Saunier

◆ Catch the individual doing things right, this helps morale
◆ Establish symbols of success and reward; offer rewards only for what you and the organisation is trying to achieve or express, e.g., shared values and objectives
◆ Be direct about areas for improvement and give tangible advice and measurements of success
◆ Never compare people; everybody is different, do not create clones
◆ Prepare to listen, not to tell or sell
◆ Have a view, but make up your mind only after the discussion(s)
◆ Establish their strengths and focus on these, not their weaknesses
◆ Use real examples, not hypothetical material
◆ Be direct and clear, not vague
◆ Be sensitive, but not 'polite'

Personally, we can't help thinking 'appraisal' is the wrong word altogether. In your ideal organisation, what would you call it? And how would that new term change the relationship of the individual to bosses, to growth and development, to the organisation, even to themselves?

Towards the Voodoo Organization 4

MAKE MINE A CAREER, NOT A JOB

At that moment Elrond came out with Gandalf, and he called the Company to him. 'This is my last word ,' he said in a low voice. 'The Ring-bearer is setting out on the Quest of Mount Doom. On him alone is any charge laid: neither cast away the Ring, nor deliver it to any servant of the Enemy nor indeed let any handle it, save the members of the Company and the Council, and only then in the gravest need. The others go with him as free companions, to help him on his way. You may tarry, or come back, or turn aside into other paths, as chance allows. The further you go, the less easy it will be to withdraw; yet no oath or bond is laid on you to go further than you will. For you do not yet know the strength of the hearts, and cannot foresee what each may meet upon the road.'

'Faithless is he who says farewell when the road darkens,' said Gimli.

'Maybe,' said Elrond, 'but let him not vow to walk in the dark, who has not seen the nightfall'.
J.R.R. Tolkien, The Lord of the Rings: The Fellowship of the Ring

Far too many of us fear ending up with a career that is a series of sometimes related but usually unrelated jobs. It is never too early or too late to think career. Ask yourself how you would like to spend the third of your life that you spend at 'work'. It really is worth doing something you enjoy. This enjoyment normally means that you find it easy to focus and commit to the activities and tasks related to something you get a kick out of doing and being. This usually means that you are doing this quite well, or sometimes just brilliantly. Does it really matter if career fulfilment is achieved with one employer or a variety of jobs?

So let's start thinking career now.

Your academic qualifications or lack of them may seem the biggest influence on the career options open to you. Never fall into this traditional trap. It's about you, you and you. What do you like? What are your interests?

Create that necessary inspirational vision of where you want to be, and what you want to be doing. Keep it alive, keep it contemporary, keep it vivid, and keep it Voodoo.

Kevin Phillips, Sunderland's England forward, stacked shelves to start with but always believed his Voodoo. Charles Dunstone left school early and, from selling mobiles to his mates, launched Carphone Warehouse.

Many years ago I trained as an accountant. My parents were delighted and impressed; I was just dejected and depressed. I could do it, but my heart was not in it, I was just doing a bunch of tasks. No soul, no commitment, just work and boring work at that. I had that adolescent affliction – no clue what I wanted to do. However I felt that computers were the place to be. This was the up and coming industry and it was kicking. This new Information Technology (IT) was new, cool, well-paid and carried huge currency and cachet. But how?

Having asked around about what the organisation's IT department was up to, I wondered out loud if they needed any trainees. I found that in six months they would be advertising internally for a trainee programmer. This was circa 1980, and all of a sudden by complete accident and chance, I had lit the blue touch paper – whoosh! The green shoots of career reared their beautiful heads; I just had to keep the gardens fertile. The garden had its regular share of sunshine and manure to keep most things rosy. Nine months later, I was the only trainee programmer at the Road Transport Industry Training Board. I had arrived at the start point of a potential career and by now could write simple computer programs, but most of all, I felt hot, excited and passionate about my new found industry. Consequently, I made the age-old mistake of keeping my head down, and grafting in order to demonstrate my worth. Whenever the perception is that we have landed a plum role or position, our natural tendency is to go native, and ensure that we are worthy. At times this can mean forgetting the capability and drive that got us the position in the first place. Remember: be true to your self and your capability, it's what will get you your next position or promotion, and most of all, keep you motivated. Anyone can graft. I felt privileged to be there, and boy was I going to prove them right.

This was in the early 80s. It would have been easy to become really conscious and aware that in most of the roles and positions I found myself, I was the only black person around. There were some real issues and barriers, but nothing was going to deflect me from this massive beacon I was aiming for. Should I have found time for some other meaningful things around me? Sure, I should have. I was too busy having a great time with my embryonic career. It was target Nirvana, my own career paradise, it was everything to me. I could not escape its constant and positive attraction. Its sun shone so bright and so addictively. Every time I thought about my career path, I brought on my own natural high.

This traditional focus on having to have a career tended to mean working with an organisation for a decent amount of time, in order to have done our apprenticeships. This could mean a few years; it rarely meant a couple of months. This would be followed by progression to a practitioner's position or some supervisory position. It would certainly be a good few years before any thought of moving elsewhere would even occur. This was mainly driven by fear of failure and the belief that by staying in a position for a number of years was proof of loyalty and therefore increased market worth. The organisations would see this slightly differently. Traditionally employers provided stable, long-term jobs in return for loyalty to the company. They also promised a sense of family and belonging. Long-term employees were valued and company loyalty was the return for this investment.

The 90s saw new strategies and approaches from organisations facing increasing competition and the impact of globalisation. These honourable and comfortable relationships began falling apart, and will probably never be the same again. Employees started to feel the effect of downsizing, mergers and acquisitions, and a boom-and-bust-style economy. Jobs were no longer for life and, shockingly, organisations were not necessarily going to 'look after them' in difficult times.

These economic changes are still continuing to alter our world of work radically. Only twenty years ago job opportunities for the young and aspirational were still dominated by the traditional, salaried, Monday to Friday and 9 to 5 type jobs which promised a career. Then it started to change. This change was facilitated by the recession of the early 90s. Many permanent, full-time opportunities started to disappear, and were replaced by a combination of freelance and short-term, contract-based positions. This started to feed a new entrepreneurial culture. The brave and the desperate started to embrace this new method of working and started to manage their careers and work/life balance very differently. It had many similarities to the way businesses were run. The best contracts were in high demand, no matter how short-term; it became increasingly normal to have a number of concurrent part-time positions. Some people decided to start their own businesses with their redundancy cheques. This trend has not gone away, despite economic conditions changing yet again.

In an increasingly technology-dependent and driven world workers have to be constantly learning and studying to keep up with new technology. Industries are changing so rapidly that we now face skills shortages in many sectors, meaning employers can't find enough workers with all the skills needed to perform a job (as opposed to a labour shortage, which is not having enough people to fill vacant positions). The technology sector, for instance, is facing skills shortages, and it is predicted that the shortage will continue into the foreseeable future. Employers are looking for workers with the right combination of job-related skills and the appropriate profile.

Employers and employees have begun to develop new partnerships to serve their needs more fully in the new environment. Organisations are beginning to tailor benefit packages to the meet the needs of the individual in an aggressively competitive marketplace for talent.

As the work arrangement is more temporary and must serve the needs of both the employee and the company, prospective employees carefully examine working conditions. This is particularly apparent in the highly competitive high-tech sector.

Workers are more stressed than ever, as they have to simultaneously manage their careers whilst worrying about their contribution and performance.

The work/life balance is now a major worry as we increasingly trade off work and family. The much sort after balance has become increasingly difficult to maintain in the fast-paced competitive environment in which most people have to work.

Business now has to compete globally and employers are consequently more concerned about the costs of benefit packages, income taxes and their relationship to profits.

There will be less and less emphasis on the traditional ('we'll take care of you') values, in favour of a culture which supports shared responsibility between employers and employees. The ability to work in an environment where things change on a continuous basis is demanding a new level of robustness and a resilience to this lack of stability.

All of us have to take responsibility for our health and wealth, taking decisions to move to more favourable environments as necessary. A new and welcome focus on individual contribution is bringing new measurements of success, but also delivers a new level of stress. The onus moves clearly onto individuals to manage their work/life balance, and this becomes a key attraction for prospective employers.

This new approach has also spawned new working arrangements like virtual offices, teleworking, hot desking, home working etc. Compensation and packages are straining to keep pace with these new developments.

A new and completely different approach will be required of all organisations to compete in this new world. The competitive advantage of any organisation will be its ability to react quickly to changes in the business environment, to be responsive and able to adapt speedliy to customer demands, and to hire efficient, effective and healthy people.
This new environment also forces the individual to develop new capabilities in order to compete. Individuals now have to market themselves in a manner that has never sat comfortably

with the prevailing culture. Speaking highly about one's personal ability and prowess is no longer shocking and unacceptable. In many respects, if you do not believe in your abilities, who else will? It is vital now to maintain health and work/life balance not just as a sensible strategy, but also as a key competitive advantage for employment. It has become very clear who owns your career; in only twenty short years the Voodoo is here.

By now I too have left corporate life and joined the world of the portfolio workers. It took some time to realise how institutionalised I had become. I have begun to overcome this, and am thriving in my new world of work. My work/life balance has improved out of all recognition. However, I really do miss some of the tribal benefits of being in a team. I thrived on the camaraderie and interdependence. Building new partnerships and relationships has taken time, care and courage. It can be done. It can be fun.

At a recent conference, I was challenged by an individual who was in his seventeenth year of service for his organisation (and still gunning for that initial promotion). He felt very strongly that in my twenty years in industry, I had achieved relative success and progression by leaving organisations to move to better positions elsewhere. He viewed this as close to both cowardice and cheating. A very interesting point of view!

I asked him if he was happy in his work. He sat back down. He apparently did not feel this worthy of further comment.

There are many ways of going forward, but only one way of standing still.
Franklin D. Roosevelt

Towards the Voodoo Organization 5

OFFICE POLITICS AND CULTURE

Treebeard was very thoughtful after Gandalf had gone. He had evidently learnt a lot in a short time and was digesting it. He looked at us and said: "Hm, well, I find you are not such hasty folk as I thought. You said much less than you might, and no more than you should. Hm, this is a bundle of news and no mistake".

J.R.R. Tolkien, The Lord of the Rings: The Two Towers

The old chestnut is 'I left because I could not stand the politics'. The culture of the business or how political the business is, they tend to be one and the same thing. When we are being positive we tend to talk about culture. When we want to be quite negative we call it politics. Has anyone heard about a positive political climate in any organisation? I guess not.

What is this politics stuff? It tends to be how people behave and interact with each other in an organisation. It reflects the openness and honesty of colleagues. The amount of respect that workers have for each other. How social and welcoming the working environment is also affects our view of the politics or culture.

Cultures are man-made, not set in stone. The politics of an organisation can be influenced, changed, but rarely ignored. These are the mores and values of the organisation. When thinking about a life partner, would you ignore how they behave and what their priorities are? So why do we do this for our chosen jobs and careers?

Whilst working for Pepsi, I experienced their approach to assessment centres. They were ostensibly about recruitment, but they were much more about 'fit'. 'Fit for purpose' was the long hand, what it really meant was 'are you culturally sound for this organisation, at this time?' This was Brave New World stuff for me. It was instructive to see and feel the assessors (one for every candidate – usually 8-10) recognise and reward behaviour that would thrive in the constantly boiling cauldron that was the Pepsi culture. Up to ten candidates would be called in for a very full day that would consist of about eight exercises that they would be assessed against. The candidates would be asked to strut their stuff in front of selected Pepsi managers as assessors. Assessors tended to be tough, and businesslike. Small talk was deemed to be for small people.

Tough, focused, ambitious, and self-sufficient candidates tended to flourish. This was a hard-nosed, results-oriented machine, which was on a rapid growth strategy, and failure was not even in the Pepsi vocabulary, let alone an option. Hunters not farmers. They worked all hours on purpose and by choice. They bayoneted the wounded. Natural born winners – or were they? No, just a frighteningly well picked 'team' or, more accurately, group of talented individuals.

During the assessment centre there were role-plays, interviews, presentations, psychometric tests on reasoning and judgement, group exercises, and all candidates were even assessed during lunch. Tough, direct, uncompromising, commercial, competitive, ambitious and seriously focused were all behaviours that were looked for and universally praised. Many other behaviours and capabilities were seen, at best, as being of secondary importance.

It was well worth understanding this prior to signing up, especially in situations where there were no assessment centres giving us a vital clue.

Oh yeah, by the way, the final exercise of the assessment centre was to spend a full day with the potential team one could be working with in the future.

How many times have we asked for a pre-employment day with potential work colleagues in an everyday work environment? It might be the best day – spent with people you really do not want to be around for much longer.

An education isn't how much you have committed to memory, or even how much you know. It's being able to differentiate between what you know and what you don't.
Anatole France

Conversely:

When the doors of opportunity swing open, we must make sure we are not too drunk or too indifferent to walk through.
Jesse Jackson

The *My Voodoo* steps to acquiring the appropriate culture and avoiding those office politics when moving to a new environment are:

◆ Understand clearly what sort of working environment you thrive in

◆ Always make an informed choice about the culture you are thinking of joining

◆ Ensure you seek the views and opinions of some of the following:
     existing staff
     recent leavers
     suppliers
     competitors
     customers
     future colleagues

◆ Be prepared to walk away from a great package if the cultural climate does not embrace you

◆ Be clear that the management actually understand the culture they have and, importantly, discover if they intend to bring about any necessary change

◆ Be realistic about what sort of cultures exist, what is really acceptable and what is a deal breaker

FALSE ORDER

So neat, so calm on the surface.

Everything is so normal

So peaceful, yet inside there is no order,

There is merely nonsense.

Homework, "Help Jo, book, oh my head".

This heat! It's three a.m. Let her go.

She can't. I need her.

In the classroom false order reigns again.

Ovid. You can piece together the translation.

But the words have no meaning.

My eyes they're so tired.

My stomach's doing acrobatics.

Why now? My life was so ordered before.

What's happened?

Where's the order?

Why don't I know what I want anymore?

Why can't I make sense of anything?

No order. No peace. Chaos.

Well there is an order. A false order.

Becky Butler

We have just looked at what sort of culture you'd want to join. How about when you are in the bleak mid-winter already? What do you do when you have established that the environment is all too much for you? There are no soul mates; it is all a bit too competitive, only those who shout loud ever get noticed.

Cultures can be changed, but in my experience this is a long journey and requires major resolve and nerve for success. I have had 'hands on' experience of leading a cultural turnaround. It was not easy, and there was quite a bit of unavoidable human carnage.

Here's the story:

Prior to joining IPC Magazines, I had seven interviews with various members of the board and senior personnel (a clue about the culture there). After one particularly long session, I asked if I could see the environment where my prospective team worked. It had just gone 5pm. Arriving on the 28th floor was like visiting the Marie Celeste. The place was spotlessly tidy and certainly not inconvenienced by people. There was one member of the team left. He was polite but very nervous in my presence, and massively deferential. It gave me the impression of a team that was not under any kind of pressure, there was no sense of urgency, and there was no real drive or energy about the place. I needed to know more.

Did this tell of a well-managed and slick unit that had it all under control? Maybe they could be tell-tale signs of dipping morale and a little lack of direction. I needed to know more.

I was getting hooked on the opportunity of a turnaround. After a pre-employment meeting with the senior members of the team, it became obvious that this was a team that had become tired of straining at the leash for some useful employ. I was engaged with a bunch of excellent fire-fighters. They were brilliant at problem solving; however, this constant drain on resources and strategic thinking had established a completely reactive culture that lacked the confidence to be self-directing.

I needed to know a lot more.

This was a business that had delivered a sustained run of record profits with little or no revenue growth. This was a story of cost cutting; in fact it had become second nature. This was an extremely tightly-run business with strong operational management. It was becoming increasingly clear to the board of IPC that cost cutting alone was no longer a sustainable

strategy. The bold decision was taken to change the culture of the business and go for growth. This change was a colossal one for the business, and I believed the right one.
I was beginning to understand the culture.

Business transformation was happening simultaneously all around the organisation. This was one of my most exciting periods in business, and also one fraught with uncertainty and fear.

Did I really want to know any more? Yes.

My own specific challenge was to move the soul of the IT function to a more risk-embracing model which would enable some necessary focus on vision and strategy. Coupled with this, it was essential to establish a reputation for delivery, without which no one would listen to any philosophy about futures. I now had appropriate knowledge, but with a massive thirst for more.

In changing culture one of the most overlooked areas is language. The vernacular of the current incumbents will say a lot. A major symbol of success in changing culture is the changing language. For an IT organisation, this is a fundamental issue. The IT industry has invented its own impenetrable language, which has encouraged and fed the alchemists' aura around IT people. In a world of alchemists, we were Boots the alchemists.

Like most business functions, IT has two discrete roles. Firstly, the maintenance: the successful running of all the businesses' IT systems. This focuses on the safety and security of the business and its systems. Secondly, development: establishing an IT strategy that fully supports and, where appropriate, delivers the business strategy.

These two significantly different agendas require significantly different sub-cultures. I call these two different areas, somewhat crudely, the plumbing and the philosophy.

The plumbing is the successful day to day running of all the businesses' systems to an agreed service level. This in my view needed its main cultural attributes to be careful, thorough, practical, cautious and calm. The philosophers tend to be more enterprising, faster moving, a little more self-sufficient, demanding and a lot more difficult to manage, but a lot easier to lead.

By far the best way of changing culture is to change the people, bringing in those who consistently behave in the manner you are looking for. It is rare that we are presented with a clean slate and the opportunity to build from scratch, so when we do have the opportunity we must think about the personalities we are bringing together and not just myopically chase skills. Think culture.

The first step is a cultural audit. Who works within the team? What are their cultural habits in thinking and in language? What's valued and acted upon? What has power, what struggles? Overall, how far away is this from your desired situation?

It is imperative to understand the financial implications of any major cultural change. It may be desirable to have an over-qualified team that could do so much more. What are the salary implications? Is this the best use of that sort of capability? Raising the cost base of an organisation may be just the price that needs to be paid in order to deliver business objectives, but do not let it be a surprise.

The economics of the day (still true now), made it clear that philosophers were worth a lot more in the open market than plumbers.

It is essential not to fall into the trap of having all the measurements of success based on internal metrics. The best comparisons are made with external organisations, ideally your competitors, but definitely with organisations in your market sector, and with organisations of a similar size in any industry. The key measures to look at are salaries, number of people, profile, track record and budgets.

Be clear about what needs to be injected into the team to reach the Promised Land.

Let's get back to my team at IPC. The biggest change was to become two teams but remain as one family, with completely differing and at times conflicting objectives and therefore cultures. Given the prevailing market forces, it was going to be a heck of a challenge not to create a 'rich man, poor man' feeling. This is very difficult but eminently achievable. By consistently demonstrating and communicating how both teams are valued and their worth and importance to the overall mission, stigma can be avoided.

Without getting into the cornflakes (the myopic detail), I hit lucky with a few critical appointments:

◆ The leadership team for the plumbing was probably the pivotal decision. One of my long servers was a bit of a perfectionist who lapped up detail and wanted recognition as being excellent at his job. He was very well respected in the team and, importantly, with our customers in the business. Incidentally, the changing of users to customers was a transforming event for all concerned. Our linguistic skills were on the up! His cautious approach to his work made him the perfect candidate. His predilection for managing as opposed to leading may well have been an advantage in the formative days.

◆ Given the previous appointment there was a need for something new and keen. We appointed a manager from the BBC. He had never worked in IT, but he had managed a support desk for camera crews and the like. It was brilliant to see the impact of having someone in charge who was never deflected by the sweetness of the technology, but focused totally on the customer experience. The two of them forged a brilliantly interdependent relationship. The culture changed immediately, but took another year or so to become stabilised. There were many necessary casualties.

◆ One of the existing managers had the most amazing people skills; he described himself as a 'chronic person pleaser'. He had the respect of all customers and all members of the team. Three keyboards and screens surrounded him; approaching his desk was like seeing Liberace in his full glory. But what a guy! He had joined the company as a 17 year old and had already had over 17 years of experience. He started off in finance and 'progressed' to IT. Surprisingly, he was the entrepreneurial spirit of the team. He knew everybody; he had acquired a great understanding of all the processes and practices in the businesses. Consequently, customers trusted both his intentions and his approach. He was the man. Elevating him to the senior management team was a shot in the arm for the locals. A huge symbol of success.

◆ Another recruit had worked at some serious places, in serious roles. He had great language. He spoke in an easy manner and it was very difficult to dislike him, a bit like Kofi Anan. He had a naturally strategic mind, but in this environment one had to have credentials. He had credentials. His joining was transformational for the team, a big hitter; it is uplifting for any team to sign Beckham.

Voodoo, when first encountered feels scary, really scary

Voodoo says
everybody
deserves
feedback

♦ I needed someone who could not spell fear. He had worked for me at M&S, in fact joined as a graduate trainee. After a few years we had worked together twice and had a telepathic understanding. His ambition was quite scary. He had gone on to work for Glaxo, and was up for some action. He had more energy and drive than any Ferrari. And, as with all performance cars, bloody high maintenance, but you would want to have him on your side in any competition.

Sorry, let's slip back out of the cornflakes.

Let us just consider the differing traits I have only touched upon. What will this heady cocktail taste like? Will I be able to lead such a disparate team? Have you seen *The Seven Samurai* or *The Magnificent Seven*, maybe even *The Dirty Dozen*? Stories of how diversity breeds success.

I still needed to know more.

This felt like getting the dream team together. The theory looked sound. What about the practice? They were building their respective teams. There was a heck of a lot of change taking place simultaneously, some quite well managed, some just happening. For some of us, it was massively exciting, for others it was murderous. No stability, no structure, no order, no routine, and some of my team were really suffering. Especially the plumbers. Order was a necessity for them to succeed. This constantly changing world needed some balance.

At times like this, it is great to have some non-participant observation. Someone who is respected and trusted, but critically is independent and objective. At this stage it was time for the cavalry and I called David Firth. We had met on a boat somewhere. We both had speaking slots on this boat. I liked what he was saying, it made sense and it was radical, and quite scary.

David became part of the cultural transformation experience at IPC. As an independent consultant, he did many things for the team that I will never know about. It was imperative that he had a private and confidential relationship with the team, where they could let rip about anything and especially me. David would provide me with generic feedback without ever naming names. At times he would be telling me in no uncertain terms how I had upset or confused my team with recent communications or my behaviour. This was great and timely feedback, then it was down to me to act.

The second activity that David ran at IPC was his 'Unit of One' series of events. David had the last Friday of every month from 2pm until close to run thought-provoking sessions that were not mandatory to attend. He always had a good attendance, and I was the only person who could not turn up. The impact and effect was not what I expected. Individuals who attended started to take control of their careers, some left to do other things, some just started to enjoy their work. The natural management reaction is to switch into retention mode. People resigning is not necessarily a bad thing; in fact, managed churn is very helpful.

All in all, the culture moved from one that was definitively risk averse, reactive with alarmingly low self-esteem. It changed to a more risk-embracing approach, with a lot more confidence, better team spirit, faster moving and most of all, a track record of solid delivery.

Tellingly, enjoyment came back in vogue.

Voodoo asks why predict the future when you can make it?

However, there were some drawbacks in moving so quickly to change culture. We spent a long time living with ambiguity; should it be 'the the old way that we know best' or 'this new way that feels quite risky'? – this was the oft-engaged debate. A lack of structure and process existed for longer than anticipated, making some members of the team feel really uncomfortable.

The creation of a more competitive environment was not always helpful or positive – to the individuals concerned. But that was their Voodoo, neither right or wrong.

There is always a price to pay…

Use what talent you possess: the woods would be very silent if no birds sang except those that sang best.
Henry Van Dyke

Our doubts are traitors and make us lose the good we oft might win by fearing to attempt.
William Shakespeare

Towards the Voodoo Organization 6

MENTORING

" I have been so caught up in the thoughts of leaving Bag End, and of saying farewell, that I have never even considered the direction" said Frodo. "For when am I to go? And by what shall I steer? What is to be my quest? Bilbo went to find treasure, there and back again; but I go to lose one, and not return, as far as I can see".

"But you cannot see very far," said Gandalf. "Neither can I. It may be your task to find Cracks of Doom; but that quest maybe for others: I do not know. At any rate you are not ready for that road yet".

"No indeed!" said Frodo. "But in the meantime what course am I to take?"

"Toward danger; but not too rashly, nor too straight", answered the wizard. "If you want to take my advice, make for Rivendell. That journey should not prove too perilous, though the Road is less easy than it was, and it will grow worse as the year fails".

"Rivendell!" said Frodo. "Very good: I will go east, and will make for Rivendell".

J.R.R. Tolkien, The Lord of the Rings: The Fellowship of the Ring

Life can be the most vibrant gift in the world. Many of us are optimists who feel positive about most issues and opportunities but no matter how optimistic an individual can be, on occasion we can all feel lost and pessimistic about our lot. This can be because of life's general travails or because the job is just getting on top of us. What do we do? Where can we go? Who can we talk to? Where is that friendly voice that not only knows me well but, vitally, cares for me and wants me to succeed?

In my experience this is a regular occurrence, especially career-wise. I have been extremely fortunate to have a mentor or two at hand. These mentoring relationships do not happen by chance. I have arranged or engineered them.

But let us start at the beginning. Everybody deserves feedback. Feedback generally comes when we could really do without it, and in our world it tends to be negative and rarely given in good humour. We have all become really adept at catching people doing things wrong! Just ask yourself how you feel when you receive positive feedback from someone you really admire and respect.

This is powerful stuff, but rare and hardly ever delivered by design and on a regular basis. The beauty of this 'catching you doing things right' is that it makes us far more open and receptive to our areas for improvement, especially from someone whose opinions you hold in high esteem.

Whilst working for Marks and Spencer at its peak in the late 80s and early 90s, I soon realised that nearly all the members of the board of directors and the majority of the senior executives in the company were all ex-merchandisers. I worked in the ultimate service department, Information Technology (IT). We were never seen as business partners, this was serious service provision. Every time I hear 'service provision', it reminds me of working on a plantation. It was obvious to me, a seriously ambitious person, that I had to have a complete understanding of the merchandising experience in order to progress to a significant role within the organisation. But how?

At this stage in my career I had never heard about mentoring; I do not think it had become corporate lingua franca. I decided that I needed to get myself an attachment or secondment to a merchandiser's position. I did not even know or understand what a merchandiser did. There was only one way forward. Identify a seasoned expert who had progressed to a senior position within the company. They would easily identify what was so important about the role of a merchandiser and importantly, what capabilities this experience provided for a senior executive at M&S.

There was only one place to start, at the top, the board of directors. I did not know any of them. I looked at the next layer down, and I recognised the names of the IT executives, but not much else. I recognised Jack (we will refer to him as Jack). I had been in the audience at a presentation he led about buying strategy for Ladies' Wear. I remember him being affable and personable, and very clear about the strategy, but most of all, having a great touch with his people. It was a seriously uplifting experience, and I felt the whole audience wanted to deliver, as much for him as themselves and the company.

When I asked around about Jack, he was a regular local hero. I needed to speak to him. I needed to understand what made him tick. I needed to know. I wanted to know. I needed help. His help. There was only one thing to do.

Those eyes are gorgeous I must advance.
Finlay Quaye

Contact Jack. Easier said than done. At M&S, he was as close to God as my imagination could take me. I needed an intermediary. I knew his personnel manager. Game on.

She arranged a short meeting where I could 'accidentally' meet Jack. Desire burned really brightly, ambition burned even brighter; fear was a virtual waterfall on my fires of ambition.

After ten minutes of arriving, I was talking to Jack, five minutes later we had agreed to have lunch and chat. Jack was a brilliant mentor.

We met once a month. It was the meeting and moment I looked forward to most. He was generous and gave me a damn good listening to, and how he listened. He heard every stutter, every hesitation and boy, did he get to know me. When he spoke it was always friendly, calming but invariably correct. He knew everything about M&S. He saw all the hurdles I never knew existed. He gave me a confidence and assurance that was just special. Most of all, he told me the truth. I felt really comfortable hearing about my poor judgement, mistakes and lack of experience. He always gave me serious and directional feedback with some great hints and tips on how I could move forward. What a guy, what a mentor.

Our relationship endured; it was private, and it was personal and great mutual fun. The only measurement of success, and reason for carrying on, was that we both wanted to carry on meeting. Simple really.

What I did not realise was how much of a two-way street mentoring really is. Mentors get a lot out of it, which is one of the major reasons why they do it, and are so good at it. Most people want to be associated with success, especially if they can look back and say 'I played a part in making that person what they are today.'

Secondly, mentors get to see their thoughts and strategies played out by a willing accomplice who might well turn a previous situation, which the mentor never managed to handle well, into a minor triumph. The mentor can live this as if they were actually there.

At times there is the opportunity for role reversal.

Jack and I lost each other for a while when I left M&S. We got back together 7 years later. By then I had moved onto the board of Pizza Hut for three years and gone on to the board of IPC Magazines. I had heard through friends and the media that things were not going well at Marks and Spencer, and the 'old guard' were in the firing line.

Ladies' Wear seemed to be under the spotlight as the major under-performer and Jack, as head of Ladies' Wear, was being wrapped up as Mr Blame. I contacted Jack and arranged a mentoring lunch at his place. We had lunch in his office and he was still as personable and caring as ever. I did notice that he did not have the same bounce in his step and he looked really tired. Without noticing it or planning it, he was doing the talking and I was listening. He needed support. He trusted the company. He was convinced that the company always did what was best for its people.

We met once more at my offices at IPC Magazines and had lunch on the 29th floor. We spent a long time gazing across the beautiful city of London. The panorama seemed to suit a rather melancholy lunch. Jack had had enough, he never said as much, he never had to. I too agreed with him that he had other great things to achieve, and that there certainly was life after M&S.

A massive guy, and a massively beneficial experience.

Jack taught me so many things. I learned, through my close proximity, just by seeing him in action. For one of my very first sessions he invited me to sit next to him at the Lingerie review. This was where next season's designs and colours were first modelled to the department's full hierarchy. First and foremost, most men in the organisation would have given their right arms to be there, but far more importantly, it was a master class in giving necessary feedback, whilst constantly building team morale.

It is a real shame that the Jacks of this world are ever lost to us. Everybody needs a mentor at some time, and Jack was one of the best people I ever had the joy to meet and work for. Perhaps the sorcerer's apprentice was now becoming a sorcerer himself.

Funnily enough, as we went to print, there was an interesting piece in Fast Company magazine by Harriet Rubin, one of their chief correspondents, called 'The Trouble with Mentors'. Here's a whiplash-fast tour through her piece, maybe as a counterpoint to René's experiences. Harriet reminds us of six main points on mentoring:

Before you learn what others know, you need to learn what you know...

If there is someone whose knowledge you need, offer to help that person...

Cultivate relationships with important people before you need them...

Make sure the deal is reciprocal: never underestimate what you have to give...

Say goodbye before the relationship stops giving...

The world itself is the best teacher...

Generating the Voodoo Organisation

In the Voodoo world, finding the right questions is often more powerful than finding the best answers (since the 'best answer' your company grasps at in order to get itself out of the confusing and uncomfortable world of paradox and complexity may be a 'best answer' short of what's really needed).

So for those of you bent on making magic happen around you in your company, here are some 'right questions'…

They apply whether you're starting a company from scratch, whether you're part of a small team in a huge organisation, or whether you are 'outside work', engaged in a community group.

The courage is only in asking them.

QUESTIONS THAT HELP GENERATE A VOODOO ORGANISATION

Why are we driven to do this?

Do we all believe we can do this?

What self-knowledge or guiding principles give us faith we can do this?

Who are our Sorcerers (or mentors) for this undertaking?

What is work for in the human experience?

What is the role of business in the world?

What are bosses for?

What's going on in our business environment, now and in the future?

What business are we in?

What promise do we offer to our various stakeholders?

Why would they give a damn?

What does success look like?

Who may be harmed by our endeavours?

By what metrics will we measure our performance?

What experiences have we had in other companies which we will commit to un-creating here?

What work will be created by the delivery of this promise, and what processes and systems will we have to enable that work?

What information will be generated through this work and how will we capture, understand and utilise this information?

What relationships will be created by these systems and processes?

What processes will we use to enable our relationships?

What is in the Universal Job Description for this company?

What do we understand about keeping the fire burning?

How many chairs will we need?

And some questions for the leader or driver of this project alone:

Why am I doing this?

What are the possible consequences of my actions?

What do I most hide from?

QUESTIONS FOR REINVIGORATING YOUR TEAM

LOOKING BACK

What did we do last year? Month by month can we recollect what happened, where we focused, who came, who went?

How did it feel last year? Could we plot, month by month, a morale graph?

If last year were a movie or a novel, what genre would it be?
What is title of this movie or novel?

How has this department changed over the year?
For example:

> structure
> priorities/driving ideas
> skills
> type of people

How has it stayed the same?
What have been the biggest learning points of the year – mistakes and successes?

Is it learning those lessons?
What should it be most proud of?

What should it be most frustrated by?

If you could make a wish for this team, what would it be?

LOOKING FORWARD

What movie do we want to make for the coming year?

What will we name it?

What are our priorities for the year?

What are our 3-5 major goals this year and how will we measure their achievement?

What do we know about ourselves (our habits, our tendencies) that might get in the way of us achieving them – and how can we utilise that knowledge so that we reach our goals?

VOODOO CHECKLIST REVISITED 2: THE TEN GOLDEN PRINCIPLES FOR A VOODOO ORGANISATION

◆ Consider: How does what you do improve your customers' lives? People want their lives to be better – easier, smoother, happier, more peaceful, richer – than now. Can they get it elsewhere? The more they can only get it from you, from your own unique fingerprint on your product or service, the more they need it.

◆ Your customers always want more than you think they do. Offer wide as well as deep. Change to match your customers as they change.

◆ You must hire help who will expand the promise beyond you, not replicate it on behalf of you. That requires fearlessness and love on your part.

◆ Above all, people (your staff, your customers) seek meaning. Give them a meaning (a goal, a purpose, a calling, a promise).

◆ Deliver. Make everything you imagine real.

◆ Nothing can be done well on your own, even masturbation. How rich is your network of influences, mentors, capabilities? And how rich is their network? That sum is how rich you are.

◆ Delve deep to find out what really makes the difference, for you and then for others. Focus there.

◆ Connection is a promise in a lonely world, a tool, and a process. You have to keep working at it. You have to put in to connection with your customers, your people, your self, what you dream to get out.

◆ Change the world by all means, but you'll only know how to do that by having an intimate and constantly updated understanding of how it currently seems to work – what currently seems to drive it, and what it appears to be lacking.

◆ Never fool yourself that things will always tie themselves up into easily memorable prescriptions, or that promises will come true. Life's a mess. Adapt. Make it up.

And you'll always learn another equally powerful insight, if you listen.

Voodoo in the World Part One:

VOODOO IN BUSINESS

FAST AND SLOW: a look back and a look ahead

In *Corporate Voodoo* we looked at some role model businesses for the new millennium, and we called these Fast businesses. We also looked at some businesses that we felt were the laggards and we called these Slow businesses. In the analysis of their behaviours some organisations felt less than flattered, and some individuals from these companies felt so strongly that they had to let me know what they thought of my thoughts and me. I have always said that everybody deserves feedback, and I enjoyed both speaking and emailing with them. I also had the opportunity to visit and speak to a number of companies that we wrote about.

I have been challenged and encouraged to provide an update on these companies, especially by some ex-colleagues at Marks and Spencer.

Just to address a couple of comments we have heard. Firstly, we wrote *Corporate Voodoo* in a real time, contemporary manner by design. It was important to capture the prevailing mood and spirit of what was good and directional in business and also what was looking decidedly tired at the time. Times change, and we all need to be aware that things are moving on. This leaves us open to the 'fashionistas' jibe, but that's OK, we are not writing a historical tome, this is about now. Business and life waits for no one. It must be said that no organisation is doomed to abject failure, but the medicine may be really painful, especially if we wait until the patient is coughing up blood.

So here is a small review of our Fast and Slow businesses plus a couple to look out for.

And remember, business is personal. On reading these essays on Slow and Fast Businesses, consider your own Voodoo Questions in relation to them. In what ways are you a Marks and Spencer? In what ways do you need to do to yourself what Peter Davis is doing at Sainsbury's? And so on…

Where are they now?

SLOW BUSINESSES

Marks and Spencer

M&S have taken some really awful medicine and have not spat it out. With the recent retirement of Robert Colville (the finance director), the board has now been totally revamped. It is to the cost of the business that they waited until they had nowhere else to hide prior to taking the oxyacetylene equipment to the board of directors. This has been costly in just about every way imaginable. It is much better to manage churn than to be the victim of churn, no matter how painful. Succession plans are really necessary and they do work. Much has been achieved in a very challenging marketplace, and in the full glare of publicity. It did not have to be like this.

First and foremost, they have brought in some tremendous talent from outside at all levels. This initially caused even more turbulence. Huge changes in personnel were necessary and the cull is not over yet, but they are not shirking the task. This, however, does bring some worrying short-term de-skilling of the workforce. When this occurs simultaneously with changes in business processes and cultural behaviour, then it is surely a necessary evil and will take some time to bear fruits, but I am sure that taking all the painful medicine in one gulp is better than many sips.

The stores are beginning to look and feel different, and most of all there has been a tremendous improvement in the items on sale. This has been reflected in their improved sales and a resurgent share price. This turnaround has been very painful and it is not over yet, but in talking to people that work there, it has been – yes – extremely hurtful, but it has also been exhilarating. The confidence is coming back and there are many symbols of success.

This is pleasing for many long-term fans of this British institution, but did so many have to lose their jobs? The property portfolio has been taken to task. The Head Office is being moved to Paddington Basin to escape the awesome and powerful pull of the past. The board of directors is unrecognisable from only two years ago. Most of all, the big-hitting cavalry has come in and has started removing the grey clouds of sloth and fear from above the teams who are enjoying their new found empowerment and freedom. Yes, it probably had to be quite savage and direct.

The only real mistake is the one from which we learn nothing.
John Powell

Voodoo says: if you have to eat shit, don't nibble

BT

Even BT has taken some tough messages on board. They have not been as wholescale as Marks and Spencer, but again, things are getting better, slowly. The recently appointed chairman, Sir Christopher Bland, has taken the scalpel to the board of directors. They appear to be doing some good things about the outrageous debt mountain they accumulated. This still needs a lot of focus. The new CEO, Ben Verwaayen, has started to review the overall strategy, and it is beginning to feel right. However, the big challenges are still to do with the ponderous way they respond to challenge and opportunity. Their approach to their customers is still that of a monopoly supplier. They must also look seriously at the culture of BT. There are still far too many hobbyists, who just love being around technology, and most of all, they must start thinking customer, not job.

I am still not convinced that BT are out of intensive care, but it is not as bleak as it was a year ago.

To the man who only has a hammer in the toolkit, every problem looks like a nail.
Abraham Maslow

Can you learn without pain?

They say people are change resistant. Nonsense. People adapt very quickly – they often adapt most cleverly to subdue the discomfort they're feeling. That's why so many people carry on in jobs they hate, in relationships that they no longer cherish.

BT and M&S waited a long time before they took action. Are you doing the same?

NatWest

The changes at NatWest have been quite spectacular. Again, customer service has a long way to go, but one could say that about the majority of our high street banks. The acquisition by Royal Bank of Scotland has already started to more than pay off. They are well ahead of schedule in terms of streamlining the business, and providing fast-moving and decisive leadership. The provision of sharp and focused leadership, coupled with a clear vision and a willing workforce can achieve the seemingly unachievable. Royal Bank of Scotland are now eyeing the next target for acquisition, and I would place a good amount of money on their ability to deliver.

Both tears and sweat are salty, but they render a different result. Tears will get you sympathy; sweat will get you change.
Jesse Jackson

John Lewis

I probably received the most dissention over my choice of John Lewis as a Slow business, especially from men! I said at a recent conference (amongst other less than flattering items) that John Lewis were never knowingly open on Mondays. A senior buyer from John Lewis was in the audience and took major issue with me. He was erudite and hugely loyal, and wanted to point out that all staff (partners) are consulted regularly on whether they should open on Mondays, and surprisingly they always rejected this initiative. Someone in the audience asked whether they had ever thought of asking their customers.

I am pleased that women make nearly 80% of retail buying decisions in the UK. Women tend to be more discerning buyers and are more likely to either buy on impulse or change brands in the light of overwhelming evidence. Us men on the other hand are relatively lazy, and therefore tend to be loyal to brands we have engaged with for years. John Lewis still needs to communicate better with its customers and understand how they really feel.

However, there are some exciting initiatives at John Lewis. The launch of its new home shopping business, Ocado, will be instructive for their ability to both lead and move with pace and courage. They have also begun to bring in some seriously talented people from outside who are starting to ask uncomfortable questions. This is long overdue, especially given their recent less-than-sparkling results.

Reasonable people adapt themselves to the world. Unreasonable people attempt to adapt the world to themselves. All progress, therefore, depends on unreasonable people.
George Bernard Shaw

One way Slow businesses can speed up is by bringing in outsiders, to challenge their closed cultures.

Who do you know that would give you the most challenging advice (rather than the advice you'd most happy to hear)?

Overall, none of the chosen Slow businesses have stood still. In the case of M&S, their open-heart surgery has taken place in the most public of manners, which whilst painful has taken a lot of stakeholders with them. They are now the recipients of lots of goodwill. We wish them well.

NatWest is well on the way to becoming a star of the Royal Bank of Scotland's burgeoning portfolio.

BT and John Lewis have both moved but there is a long way to go. BT is open to public scrutiny and there are still many unbelievers, unfortunately many of these still work for the company. John Lewis still has strong support, but it is timely to see some evidence of real thrust and customer focus.

The problem is not that there are problems. The problem is expecting otherwise and thinking that having problems is a problem.
Theodore Rubin

FAST BUSINESSES

We looked at Vodafone, Orange, Dixons, Tesco and Virgin Atlantic in *Corporate Voodoo*. None of these could ever be accused of standing still. The much-reported turbulence in the telecoms industry has caused untold problems for all direct and indirect players in this marketplace.

Vodafone and Orange remain Lords of the Rings despite this volatility. Both companies have gone through major change; lets take a brief glimpse at Orange.

Orange has gone through a large number of fundamental shifts over the past couple of years. The changes in its ownership through acquisition must have an impact on its culture. Orange has been, from its inception in 1994, the most innovative player in its sector and has had the most vibrant brand. The recent takeover by France Telecom could well be the most significant. The most positive influence to date has been the rapid move to take the brand global. A perceived focus on driving revenues and, importantly, profit has seen some sparkling trading results from Orange. We have also seen the recent departure of Hans Snook, the eccentric, unorthodox, but quite brilliant inspiration behind Orange. Has this shift in culture spelt the end of the mavericks and magicians who achieved such startling growth in such a short period of time? Or is this just the necessary growing up of a successful start up that is now going through the growing pains of becoming a corporate? Many of the mavericks have made a tidy pile out of the capital events at Orange. Have they lost their verve and hunger? We will watch with interest as the story unfurls.

Vodafone has moved its strategy away from growth by market share to focusing on generating revenues and driving profitability. The CEO, Sir Christopher Gent, said at a conference recently that Vodafone has built an extremely competitive culture by design. Many were surprised that internal competition could be seen as helpful let alone desirable. One only has to look at the staggering growth of Vodafone to understand at least one benefit of this approach. How sustainable is a fairly aggressive and robust culture? What are the long-term implications of this style?

> Maybe the challenge for you won't be in awakening your passion for change – but in maintaining that passion. What do you know about yourself that will cause that passion (and the natural momentum it brings) to diminish – and how can you work against that habit resurfacing?

Different styles of leadership and culture are appropriate for the different eras for organisations. Sometimes a more hunting-based style is appropriate, usually during fierce competition or rapid expansion. Smart organisations manage the transition with great care, determination and polish. This brings us nicely to Tesco. The transition from Lord MacLaurin to Terry Leahy appeared seamless, and the success has just continued uninterrupted.

Tesco, who we have heard called The Easy Shopping Company, really are. They have turned their guns to the continent and have made a few mistakes, but you better believe that they rarely make the same mistake twice. They delivered a billion pounds sterling in profit, and are still going for growth. They now have a vision for delivering a five billion pound profit in the next few years. They will do this. Tesco now employs 235,000 people. In order to deliver this new and chilling target, they will need approximately a million members of staff! Demographics, and the different attitudes to work of generation X, has seen staff turnover increase for many large employers. Five years ago, the average length of service for Tesco employees was 10.7 years; it is now 2.8 years. Voodoo is comfortable with managed change and new talent can provide new impetus, but this rate of change can be debilitating. Tesco are well on top of this. They have had a Director of Customer Insight for a number of years now. This has definitely helped give them such an edge with their best in class customer strategies and execution. They have recently appointed a Director of People Insight. This role will look at what where the future talent will come from, and will also understand where the talent has come from in the past. Very impressive, unsurprisingly.

Two very different businesses have caught my eye recently as doing things differently and delivering the results to match their bold approaches. Ryanair have taken the aviation market by storm. From large losses just a few years ago, they are now breathing down the necks of all of Europe's full-service airlines, who are running scared of this impetuous and belligerent upstart. Michael O'Leary, the unorthodox but quite brilliant CEO of Ryanair, believes that they have hardly started.

Sainsbury's, the lumbering old stalwart of the retailing high street, has taken such a pounding from just about every quarter that many felt it really was all over. Don't you believe it! Sir Peter Davis has been cathartic for the business. There have been new appointments from the top and all the way through the organisation. They have taken the decision to move to new premises in Holborn, London. These new offices bear absolutely no resemblance to the previous outhouses gathered in and around Blackfriars, London. An open plan building, with directors located on the same floor as their teams, I know it seems desperately obvious, but most good ideas are. The surroundings are light, spacious and most of all feel positive. There is a new pace and energy. Not all of the talent that has been unleashed is new, but importantly, a large number of people have left.

Recent trading results have given some encouragement to the vision and strategy, but most of all to the culture that they are building. These are early days, but exciting days.

We intend watching these Fast businesses over the coming months with a view to identifying how their own Voodoos will differ and deliver in the future. And we'll comment upon them in future Voodoo Volumes.

Whenever you find yourself on the side of the majority, it's time to pause and reflect.
Mark Twain

The cynic knows the price of everything and the value of nothing.
Oscar Wilde, Lady Windemere's Fan

How do these apparently opposing quotations apply to you?

Voodoo in the World Part Two:

VOODOO AT HOME

(I) RELATIONSHIPS

'Any Elf that comes with you will be welcome,' said Treebeard.

'The friend I speak of is not an Elf,' said Legolas; 'I mean Gimli, Glóin's son here.' Gimli bowed low, and the axe slipped from his belt and clattered on the ground.

'Hoom, hm! Ah now,' said Treebeard, looking dark-eyed at him. 'A dwarf and an axe bearer! Hoom! I have good will to Elves; but you ask much. This is a strange friendship!'

'Strange it may seem,' said Legolas; 'but while Gimli lives I shall not come to Fangorn alone. His axe is not for trees, but for orc-necks, O Fangorn, Master of Fangorn's Wood. Forty-two he hewed in the battle.'

J.R.R. Tolkien, The Lord of the Rings: The Two Towers

The Yearning

30% of people married six to nine years yearn to be single again, says a survey in the paper today.

25% of these people say the lesson they have learned from marriage is 'never again'.

A Reader's Digest MORI poll says an estimated 40% of marriages now head for divorce.

Home alone

The number of Britons living alone has doubled in 30 years.

Almost a third of households now consist of just one person. The statistics from the Government's 2000 General Household Survey highlight the decline of the traditional family.

While all age groups have been affected by rising divorce rates, the young are increasingly choosing to be on their own. Thirty years ago 92% of families consisted of couples in a stable relationship. This has been falling to 74%. Single mothers are up from 7% to 23% and lone fathers from 1% to 3%. The number of women who do not marry their child's father rose from 1% to 11%.

Just 54% of men and 51% of woman are now married.

Till death us do part

Research indicates that divorce has now become a major killer of middle-aged men.

Men who go through a divorce are almost a third more likely to die within ten years than men who stay married, government figures showed last month.

And while marriage has long been known to be associated with good health for men, the study suggested that divorce is much more dangerous than staying single or being left a widower.

Figures, calculated by the Office for National Statistics, ring alarm bells; they show that a man who divorces is at a 31% greater risk of death within ten years than one who stays married.

Are we still up for relationships?

What are relationships like today? The figures above tell us that in the same way we are leaving companies a lot more readily than we did many years ago, so now relationships are subject to a similar churn and 'rate of attrition'. Does this matter? Surely it is just about being happy, and if you are not happy, get on with it and get out of it. Is it really that straightforward?

What about loyalty? What of the capacity for accepting and learning from difficulties and challenges? Of going deeper to solve problems rather than seeking to escape them?

Are we all subject to the MTV attention span?

Is there anything that we will not change for a better brand? Consumerism and the impulse buy are creeping into the relationship arena.

What has changed? Just about everything, actually. As we can see from the figures, some of the trends are fairly new, but still striking. The stigma associated with both not being married and getting divorced has diminished beyond recognition. This is rarely now an issue when thinking about one's happiness. Can you remember when people used to say 'I hate working here, but I have only done nine months. I am definitely leaving but I need to do 18 months to make my CV look OK'? This kind of statement is becoming less common, in fact in line with the lack of loyalty to relationships. It has been said recently that we change our life partners more frequently than we change our bank accounts. Is this really the right priority?

Is everything about convenience and speed? We want it and we want it now. We no longer need to compromise. There is choice like we have never seen before. In fact we have never had it so good, or is that really so? In a world of brands, logos, marketing, advertising are we being heavily manipulated the way Naomi Klein would have us believe in her seminal book, *No Logo*, or is this the real zero tolerance that we have created?

Perhaps our fixation with choice and personalisation is behind the statistics. We are far more selfish than we have ever been. Relationships are becoming disposable in our fast moving and fast changing world. Is this the future? One would think that there is something very positive about being more accountable for our feelings and behaviours. This must force us to be more honest about our likes and dislikes.

Voodoo says: relationships are not just for Christmas, birthdays or funerals

Is the only constant change? This can be debilitating for all relationships, partners, friends and importantly children. Is there a another, Voodoo, way?

(II) CHOOSING THE RIGHT SCHOOL

Frodo was now safe in the Last Homely House east of the Sea. That house was, as Bilbo had long ago reported, 'a perfect house, whether you like food or sleep or story-telling or singing, or just sitting and thinking best, or a pleasant mixture of them all'. Merely to be there was a cure for weariness, fear, and sadness.

J.R.R. Tolkien, The Lord of the Rings: The Fellowship of the Ring

As we explored in *Corporate Voodoo*, education is the bedrock from which many important issues and opportunities spring and are built upon in the future. Conversely, if education is not good enough, life can become an exercise in how well one can limp: sprinting is not an option. The appreciation of diversity is such an important quality in all our lives, and this definitely is developed during our school years. There is a terrific opportunity to dispel ignorance and myths about our multi-ethnic, multi-religious, different 'walks of life' society. Given the recent trials of our society – from the deeply concerning racial conflicts that exploded in Bolton, Leeds and Oldham to the desperate tragedy of September 11th 2001, from the furore around asylum seekers to our engagement with all that is European or not – it is clear that there is a need in our time for understanding, acceptance and engagement that will be imperative to building a better Britain.

One of the toughest and most complex decisions we have to take, as parents or guardians, is which school we send our children to. For many of us, we do not feel we always have a choice or we can feel that none of the choices open to us are ideal.

For a large number of us, schooling and the choice of school is still all about academia. Without a doubt academia is important, but at least of equal importance is the environment our children are learning and growing up in. School and education have a huge impact on who we are and who we will become. Many of us have turned to the league tables that nearly all of the newspapers publish to assist our thoughts and desires. This has led to overwhelming demand for places at the 'high performing' schools and huge under-subscription at those nearer the bottom of the list. This will in time become self-fulfilling, and perhaps some excellent places of learning and development may become lost to us forever.

There are a multitude of differing criteria to be taken into consideration when thinking about which school: co-educational or single sex, private or state school, local or distant, boarding or day school, specialist schools (drama, art etc.), religious, and a lot more as well. It's not just about exams and results, it's about honouring the children.

We believe it all should start with your child. Firstly, a full understanding of what makes them tick, even at an early age. These are straightforward things like what their likes and dislikes are; just like adults, children tend to enjoy what they are best at or have a major interest in. How gregarious or shy are they? How sporting are they?

I had myopically gone through all the lists in all the papers, set up a spreadsheet and ranked all the schools on some sort of academic algorithm, and could spend hours 'fixing' the results to the school I really wanted my daughter to go to. Wrong!

Living in St Johns Wood in Central London, the hugely academically-biased schools of Hampstead were my target. I had omitted to talk to two seriously important constituencies who had a vested interest in the right school. Firstly my daughter, who was amazingly well informed about the local roster of schools, and just as well briefed on the slightly more widespread options. She had friends and knew older girls who had gone on to a whole variety of schools. She had heard the horror stories of regimental approaches and she also had the stories of dreamland, where school was a bag of laughs and adventures. Ignore the children at your peril; they are very well informed indeed. They are also adept at brokering conversations with the parents of pupils who are going to the schools they really want to attend; this is seriously worth following up on.

The other extremely useful resource is the head of their current school, or nursery. A chance conversation with the head of her school, where I vented my frustrations at the huge numbers of children trying to get into the hallowed grounds of the 'top of the list' schools in our immediate area, was seriously unfair. He asked me so gently why I felt my daughter would thrive or even enjoy a fairly rigorous and austere academic environment. Initially I thought 'this guy just does not get it'. It was I who did not get it!

I was naïve about the amount of knowledge and guidance her teachers could provide. They had keen interest in her success and fulfilment throughout her educational career.

There are no correct answers or conclusions. It was more about identifying the positive ingredients for an enjoyable time and atmosphere for their growth and development.

I can remember the immediate impressions the various schools we visited made on us. From stark, severe and clinical, to some more warm, bright and engaging.

The head teacher is pivotal in any decision-making. Initially I thought the schools that offered the best salaries to teachers would attract the best teachers and consequently create the best schools. This has an obvious grain of truth. However, the real truth is that the best teachers wanted to work and deliver in a supportive and progressive environment. This environment was mainly influenced by the calibre and quality of the head teacher. This, in the main, was more important than the contents of the monthly pay-cheque.

My daughter and I attended a number of school visits and she laboured through a prodigious number of entrance exams. I completely misread and underestimated the impact of failing to receive an offer letter on my daughter. She had become a product of academic success as the only real and important measurement of her self-worth. She was devastated. I was devastated. She was being measured for skills only; all schools to date had missed any contribution made by personality.

Voodoo says: think personality not skills

When we walked into the Royal School we were met by a couple of uniformed, giggling girls who instantly engaged and stole my daughter away. They were called to stop running, and they hobbled ever so quickly out of view to give her the 'unofficial' school tour.

The head of the school was both warm and forthright about the school and its philosophy. My daughter attacked the exam with gusto and breezed it.

We have been introduced to a huge variety of her schoolmates who have had sleepovers and slumber parties at each others' houses. Meeting each other's families and getting to know each other's cultures.

It has been a great learning for all of us. The appropriate school has educated parents, teachers, and pupils.

Voodoo children are great teachers – if only we can hear

I say to you today, my friends, that in spite of the difficulties and frustrations of the moment, I still have a dream. It is a dream deeply rooted in the American dream.

I have a dream that one day this nation will rise up and live out the true meaning of its creed: "We hold these truths to be self-evident: that all men are created equal."

I have a dream that one day on the red hills of Georgia the sons of former slaves and the sons of former slave owners will be able to sit down together at a table of brotherhood.

I have a dream that one day even the state of Mississippi, a desert state, sweltering with the heat of injustice and oppression, will be transformed into an oasis of freedom and justice.

I have a dream that my four children will one day live in a nation where they will not be judged by the colour of their skin but by the content of their character.

I have a dream today.

I have a dream that one day the state of Alabama, whose governor's lips are presently dripping with the words of interposition and nullification, will be transformed into a situation where little black boys and black girls will be able to join hands with little white boys and white girls and walk together as sisters and brothers.

I have a dream today.
Martin Luther King, Jr., August 28th 1963

Endpiece

VOODOO DREAMS

What a tale we have been in, Mr. Frodo, haven't we?'
J.R.R. Tolkien, The Lord of the Rings: The Return of the King

Voodoo Asks: Is this the Future?

The Prime Minister had every right to be proud of her government's performance over the past few years especially after the problems of 2008. They were indeed helping people to make the best of their increasingly complex lives. The introduction of the smart card ID cards was working. Whilst the really cynical were feeling Big Brother was stalking them, for most of us, it was just the most brilliant time-saver from heaven. The filling in of forms was a thing of the past, loyalty points, no signatures, and most of all, no need for cash or credit cards – just brilliant.

The protests and demonstrations of the early part of this century have gone away. Direct action is a thing of the past. Without those brave protestors perhaps we would not have such a caring government, and perhaps the emergence of the corporate citizenship programmes were also down to their stance and maybe courage. All individuals are aware of their rights, but there is hardly ever the need to shout, the press are positive and vigilant champions of human and civil rights. European legislation has worked brilliantly and their partnership with the media has created an openness and transparency, which in turn has helped create an atmosphere of trust.

Expectations for customer service are higher than ever, and in the main we live in a society where businesses and the public sector are very responsive, and accountability has become second nature.

So what ever happened to the fully empowered consumer, who voted with wallets and purses? Well apart from the fact that everything is paid for by ID card since 2005, Naomi Klein's No Logo society came and went. Customers need trusted partners to assist them through their complex lives and the plethora of choices they have for everything. Sharing personal data was the norm in return for great customer service. The well-informed were even selling their personal data, and the ill-informed were barricading themselves in with their precious data, which was worthless on its own. Those who did not know how to value their data were the real losers in this age. The new 'ism' is 'profilism', the discrimination on the basis of personal profiles.

Ethical supply chains were in vogue with all major companies, this raised prices but nobody appeared to really mind. Many company CEOs liked to be seen to be distributing profits to good causes and charities.

Relationships had taken yet another turn. We all wanted them again. Loyalty was now back in fashion. Churches had gone, the new places of worship were fun and weddings were the new black. They were happening everywhere, they were no longer ceremony based, they were just sheer fun, and without the vows and the uniforms, everybody wanted to do it. Had we become braver? Whatever happened to good old cynicism? When we did we find the courage to be who we wanted to be? How new is this courage thing?

Reprinted from A Voodoo Retrospective: 2012

One of the remarkable aspects of Ali's life is that, despite being a lightening rod for all sorts of emotions, he scorned most security precautions. The 1960s were times of assassinations and violence in the United States. Ali, in some quarters, was the most hated man in America. Yet he never stopped moving freely in public. In the 1970s, the violence spread throughout the world. Terrorism became the weapon of choice, for the disaffected and disenchanted. Yet Ali continued to mingle at will. I don't need no bodyguards or guns," he said often. "God is my bodyguard; Allah watches over me. If I walk into a stadium with a hundred thousand people, no human can keep someone from putting a bullet in me. But I can't be worrying about things like that. A man filled with fear don't live and don't enjoy life. So I trust in God to look after me. Allah fixes the time when all of us will be taken."

Thus, handling security for Ali often meant little more than diverting traffic and hoping for the best.

Thomas Hauser, Muhammad Ali – His Life and Times

In *My Voodoo* we have touched on relationships, real, tangible, hurting and loving relationships. The tough stuff. How about the soft stuff? How about the 'make me feel good' stuff? Time to feel. My special and feel-good message is delivered by my life hero, Muhammad Ali. A man who gave so much, who was so much, who led by being him. I was just about old enough to creep under the table in the lounge to witness his winning the world title in 1963. The lounge was filled with my father's cronies. We had one of the few black and white televisions on the street. Against all the odds, with a colossal self-belief, a natural-born winner delivered, and gave hope to the world's many underdogs. My father and his friends could not contain themselves when he won. This was not just sport.

I next remember Ali refusing the draft and eventually being stripped of his title. As far as my father and his friends were concerned, he had just been anointed. This was necessary oxygen to a drowning people. I remember his many interviews and sound bites; he made my father smile, grow, feel worthy and connected. He made us all feel worthy, positive and connected. He was *our* champion. He was our hope, our joy and believe me, our inspiration. Black could be beautiful, Black could be special, Black could be inspirational. I could never begin to explain it, but I was someone. He made me feel. He excited me. I felt hot, I felt strong, I felt brave, most of all, I felt great being just me. He did this for all us, all races and all people. What a guy, and I am just proud to have been touched by him, forever.

Yes, you have flushed me out, I am an optimist. This means that on occasion I do feel seriously let down and disappointed usually by my shortcomings, but at times by the friends and relationships I have chosen. Shit happens. I am desperately keen to move on from these disappointments. It is not impossible, life is beautiful, and the majority of my relationships are beautiful. I am living a connected life, in a connected world, with connected people and my heart is getting better connected by the day.

Last night I listened to Sidney Poitier's acceptance speech for his lifetime achievement at the Academy Awards 2002. I felt the Voodoo thrill through me in an electrifying manner. His body language and demeanour spoke loud and together with his words spoke louder still:

I arrived in Hollywood at the age of 22, in a time different to today's. A time in which the odds against my standing here tonight, 53 years later, would not have fallen in my favour. Back then, no route had been established for where I was hoping to go. No pathway left in evidence for me to trace. No custom for me to follow. Yet, here I am at the end of this journey that, in 1949, would have been considered almost impossible – and in fact might never have been set in motion were there not an untold number of courageous, unselfish choices made by a handful of visionary American filmmakers, directors, writers and producers, each with a strong sense of citizen responsibility to the times in which they lived.

Each unafraid to permit their art to reflect their views and values – ethical and moral – and moreover, acknowledge them as their own. They knew the odds that stood against them and their efforts were overwhelming and likely could have proven too high to overcome.

Still those filmmakers persevered, speaking through their art to the best in all of us. And I benefited from their efforts. The industry benefited from their efforts. America benefited from their efforts and, in ways large and small, the world has also benefited from their efforts.

Therefore, with respect, I share this great honour with late Joe Mankiewicz, the late Richard Brooks, the late Ralph Nelson, the late Daryl Zanuck, the late Stanley Kramer, the Mirisch brothers, especially Walter whose friendship lies at the very heart of this moment, Guy Green,

Norman Jewison, and all others who have had a hand in altering the odds, for me and for others.

Without them, this most memorable moment would not have come to pass. And the many excellent young actors who have followed in admirable fashion might not have come, as they have, to enrich the tradition of American filmmaking, as they have. I accept this award in memory of all Afro-American actors and actresses who went before me in the difficult years. On whose shoulders I was privileged to stand to see where I might go. My love and my thanks to my wonderful, wonderful wife, my children, my grandchildren, my agent and friend Martin Baum and finally, to those audience members around the world who placed their trust in my judgement as an actor and filmmaker. I thank each of you for your support through the years."
Sidney Poitier

Sidney, you the man!

David and I have differing views on the world, in some areas we connect massively, in others we disconnect massively – that's OK, in fact it is much more; it is necessary and it's real. We hope *My Voodoo* helps and assists you. We hope it serves to make you think, to make you feel, to bring something instinctual and natural, but always positive, always hopeful, always Voodoo.

As I was saying, back to the future, relationships are back in vogue again. Why wait until 2012, let's get back involved now, at all levels:

Stop – Pause – Reflect

When were your greatest moments of happiness?

What do you need to do to make you feel the same way again, and again, and again?

STOP. WRITE IT DOWN HERE – NO, DON'T IGNORE ME:

WRITE IT DOWN LARGE.

PUT A DATE TO ACTION IT BY (WRIGGLE A LITTLE IF NEED BE).

PUT A NAME (OR NAMES) BY IT (SQUIRM A LOT, MAYBE).

WHAT WAS THE LAST MAJOR RISK YOU HAVE TAKEN WITH YOUR
HAPPINESS?
(FEEL SCARED, PERHAPS)

WHEN WILL BE THE NEXT TIME?
(FEEL REALLY SCARED)

MAY THE VOODOO BE WITH YOU

MY VOODOO, MY MAGIC

Warm black night
Pinpoints of light dance over my mind
Mysterious dancing
I'm not quite sure what will come of it
Whether it's good or not
But the spirits seem warm, you can never tell
Black magic comes at the strangest times
In my dreamtime my Voodoo comes
Sometimes the magic doesn't come
And it's painful

There are no pinpoints of light
I cannot make it come
Then the warm air engulfs me
But the warmth is different now
It's sticky and cloying, but I've learnt
This is a stage Voodoo goes through, my Voodoo
If I rest and don't try to think my Voodoo will return
You can find the light, black holes are never endless
Voodoo will come

Becky Butler

I don't have to be what you want me to be, I'm free to be who I want.
Muhammad Ali

The Last Pages

"What do you think of it so far?"
"Rubbish!"

Morecambe and Wise: the history of a gag

Of all the comedy acts produced by Britain, Morecambe and Wise are perhaps the best loved and most fondly remembered. They were the first truly great double act in Britain and, although many acts have tried to emulate them, no one has yet succeeded in replacing them in the hearts of the country. So, what was it that made their act unique? I think that the essential difference is that they made you care…

www.morecambeandwise.co.uk/biog.html

And they had a running gag. Every so often in the middle of one of their sketches Morecambe would shout

"What do you think of it so far?"

And the response, from Wise, from the studio audience, from the audience watching on TV, sometimes from Morecambe himself, was always

"Rubbish!"

I guess that it was a carry over from the days when they were not the most hugely popular act in the country, from the days when they were nobodies, truly asking for the recognition, acceptance and approval of the talent scouts. And in those early days, because they had not persevered enough to learn their craft, like all of us, they must have been, every so often, really rubbish. And then they reached a point when it was just a joke, because they weren't rubbish, anymore…

And the whole country, tens of millions of us every week, knew the punch line to the question. So often did we hear it that we were conditioned to respond, in joy:

"Rubbish!"

But that was a TV programme.

This is your life…

*The universe is full
of magical things
patiently waiting
for our wits
to grow sharper.*

Eden Phillpotts

Index

abused children 30, 32–3

abyss, the 118–19

actions have consequences 61, 65, 80–2

addiction 42

Ali, Muhammad 224, 225, 230

The Amber Spyglass 17

apathy 90

appraisals 165–8

the Arches 33–4

arrogance 139

Bainbridge, Carl 106–16

barriers, personal 86–92

Batmanghelidjh, Camila 28–9, 34–6

The Black Jacobins 47

Blaine, David 21–2

Blair, Tony 45

blame 88

Bland, Sir Christopher 204

book reviews 4–5

Box, Elvin K. 125–8

box thinking 6

brand values 157

Branson, Richard 157

British government 44–5

Brown, Gordon 44

Brown, John 162

Browne, H. Jackson 113

BT 204, 207

business

   see also Corporate Voodoo

   change management 106–16, 182–3, 185

   cultures 101–2, 129–42, 176–88

   fantasy literature 19–23

   values 129–42

   Voodoo generation 196–211

   Voodoo Spell ingredients 55–9

Butler, Becky 36, 59, 180, 230

Campbell, Heather 78

Carayol, René 137

careers 169–75

Carnegie, Andrew 154

Carphone Warehouse 170

case studies, Kids Company 32–4

'Cavaliers' 161

change

   agent of 79

   Bainbridge, Carl 106–16

   corporate 182–3, 185, 188–9

   perspective 61, 62–3

   relationships 213–15

checklists, Voodoo checklist 200

Chester the dog 80–1

chief executive officers 162–4

children 28–34, 216–20

choices 40, 56, 61, 63–4, 111, 215

Churchill, Winston 46

churn 202

coaching 107–8

Colville, Robert 202

complicity 42

consequences of actions 61, 65, 80–2

control over others 72–4

Corbin, Chris 113, 115–19

corporate change 182–3, 185

corporate culture 101–2, 129–42, 176–88

corporate values 129–42

Corporate Voodoo

   Bainbridge, Carl 109

corporate values 136, 139, 142

education 216

Fast/Slow businesses 55, 201

final checklist 153, 154

Harry Potter 17

mavericks/magicians 13

reader responses 4–5, 56, 105–46

cost cutting 181

courage 55, 56–7, 60, 61, 75–6

'crazees' 126

cultural audit 183

culture, corporate 176–88

customer-led Voodoo 56, 59

CVs 160

cynicism 90, 118

Daily Telegraph 17

Darrnel's Poem 31–2

Davis, Sir Peter 202, 210

decisiveness 158

desk trivia 120

disbelief, suspending 39

disposable relationships 214, 215

diversity, embracing 56, 58, 60

divorce rates 213, 214, 215

domination 72–4

Douglas, Kirk 60

dragons, five 86–92

drug abuse 32, 33

Dunstone, Charles 170

education 216–20

Einstein, Albert 58, 112

emails 98–104

Emerson, Ralph Waldo 111

employees 154–61, 185

employers' responsibilities 173, 174

Energis Squared 133–8, 140, 141, 142

Enron 18, 20

environmental influences 25

escape, need for 20

the Euro, joining 43–6

Evil Business 18

False Order (Becky Butler) 180

fantasy literature 17, 19

Fast businesses 201–2, 207–11

fear 115, 116

feedback 25, 58, 165–8, 190

fifteen perspectives 61–82

film stars 26–7
Firth, David 187
five dragons 86–92
Flores, Fernando 50
'The Fool' 13–14, 98, 127
'Fool's Clinic' 98–104
footballers 26–8
four ingredients 55–9
France, Anatole 178
freedom 39–47
freelancing 103
future scenario 222–4

Gandhi, Mahatma 59, 112
gangs, children 34
Gascoigne, Paul 'Gazza' 26
Gates, Bill 163
Gaye, Morgaine 120–4
General Electric Company 129–34, 136
General Household Survey 213
Gent, Sir Christopher 208
Greenbury, Richard 162
gut reactions 106–7, 110–11

Handy, Charles 165
happiness 214–15, 228–9
Harry Potter 17, 21

Hauser, Thomas 224
heart, alignment with 75–6
honesty, appraisals 166–7
Huxley, Thomas Henry 77
hypocrisy 68

ID cards 222, 223
ignorance 61, 77–8
independence 46–7
inevitability 41–2
integrity 61, 67–9, 74
interviews 161
invisible, the 19–20
IPC Magazines 181–8, 194
IT departments 106, 170, 182–8, 190

Jack and the Beanstalk 123
Jack (mentor) 191–4
Jackson, Jesse 178, 205
James, C.L.R. 46–7
job security 172–4
John Lewis 205–7
Jones, Vinnie 26–8, 29, 35

Karaoke story 1–3
karma 61, 65, 80–2
Keegan, Kevin 162–3

Keller, Helen 58
Kelly, Walt 59
Kids Company 28–34
King, Martin Luther 111, 221
Klein, Naomi 215
Koontz, Dean 81

landlord story 1–3
Lao Tzi 57
leadership
    Blair, Tony 45–6
    Energis Squared 133–4, 137
    IPC 184
    succession planning 162–4
    Tesco 209
Leahy, Terry 162, 209
life, shaping 40
'life-surfing' 117
living alone 213
Lloyd George, David 57
long hours 99–100
The Lord of the Rings 17, 169, 176, 189, 212, 216, 222
loyalty 172, 214, 215, 223

McLaurin, Ian 162
magic 14–16, 17
    business 19–23

fifteen perspectives 61–82
    generating 24, 37–8
    personal characteristics 24, 37–8
'The Magician' Tarot card 13, 14–16
magicians 208
making things happen, nine steps to 147–50
managers 72–4, 135, 141, 142, 165–8
Marks & Spencer 162, 186, 190–4, 202–3, 204
marriage 213, 215
Maslow, Abraham 204
mavericks 97–104, 127, 128, 208
mentors 113, 189–95
The Mirror (Becky Butler) 36
Monroe, Angus 162
monsters 18
Morecambe and Wise 231–2
movie stars 26–7
Mullen, Helen 143–7
My Voodoo, My Magic (Becky Butler) 230

NatWest 205, 207

New York WTC disaster 120, 121, 122, 123, 125
nine steps to making things happen 147–50
No Logo (Naomi Klein) 215

Office for National Statistics 214
office politics 176–88
O'Leary, Michael 210
openness 3, 13–53, 56, 58
Orange 207–8
organisations *see* business

pain and suffering 46–7, 79, 99–100
part-time work 172
passion 106–7, 117, 137, 138
people skills 185
Pepsi corporate culture 177–8
performance appraisals 165–8
personal aspects
    barriers 86–92
    life 212–16
    magic characteristics 24, 37–8
    personality 155, 157, 163, 219

power 61, 70–1
profiles 223
relationships 122, 212–16, 223
personnel 154–61, 185
perspectives, fifteen 61–82
Phillips, Kevin 170
Phillpotts, Eden 233
'philosophers' 183
planning 162–4, 169–75
'plumbers' 183, 186
poetry 31–2, 59, 180, 230
Poitier, Sidney 226–7
political power 61, 72–4
positive feedback 190
Powell, John 203
power 61, 70–1, 72–4
procrastination 91–2
'profilism' 223
promises 68–9
Pullman, Philip 17

Quaye, Finlay 192
questing 20
questions 9, 48, 197–8
     see also Three Voodoo
Questions

Radio Five Live 43
recruitment 154–61
reinvigorating teams 199
relationships 122, 212–16, 223
resilience 61, 78–80
responsibility 65–9, 173, 174
Ritchie, Guy 26
Robbins, Tom 85, 86
Roosevelt, Franklin D. 175
Ross, Andrew 129–43
'Roundheads' 161
routine 111, 113
Royal School 219–20
Rubin, Harriet 195
Ryanair 209–10

Sainsbury's 202, 210, 211
Saunier, Ann 168
scary talent 154–61
schools 33, 35, 216–20
self-appraisal 25
self-pity 87
self-responsibility 61, 65–9
September 11th, New York
     120, 121, 122, 123, 125
sexual abuse 32–3
Shakespeare, William 188
Shaw, George Bernard 206

skills 155, 157, 163, 185, 219
slave ships 46–7
Slow businesses 201–7
Snook, Hans 208
space, making 112
speed 99, 215
status quo, breaking 106–16
storytelling 20
stress 89
succession planning 162–4
surfing 113, 115

talent, scary 154–61
Talent Acquisition, Ten
Commitments 157–9
Tarot cards 13–16
Taylor, Damilola 34
teachers, schools 216–20
team-building 164, 185–6, 199
The Ten Commitments of
Talent Acquisition 157–9
The Ten Golden Principles for a
Voodoo Organisation 200
Tesco 209
Three Voodoo Questions 49,
     51, 52
     fifteen perspectives 61–82
     personal barriers 86–92

review 94–5
time, making 112
Time magazine cover 9, 48
Tolkien, J.R.R. 169, 176, 189,
212, 216, 222
The True Skeleton (Becky
Butler) 59
Tulgan, Bruce 166
Twain, Mark 211
12 Step Programme 67

unexplainable, the 19

values, corporate 129–42
Van Dyke, Henry 188
Verwaayen, Ben 204
virtual 55, 57
vision 142, 170
Vodafone 207–8
Voodoo checklist 200
Voodoo origins 47
A Voodoo Retrospective: 2012
     222–4
Voodoo Spell ingredients 55–9

Welch, Jack 129–30, 132
Whuyte, David 46
Wilde, Oscar 211

work/life balance 173, 175
World Trade Center 120, 121,
     122, 123, 125
worry 89
writing in this book 8

you models 7

Zukav, Gary 67